URBAN LAND INSTITUTE
Award Winning Projects 2005

Deloitte.

This book was made possible in part through the generous sponsorship of Deloitte.

URBAN LAND INSTITUTE
AWARD WINNING PROJECTS 2005

David Takesuye

Contributing author Julie Stern

ULI–the Urban Land Institute
1025 Thomas Jefferson Street, N.W.
Suite 500 West
Washington, D.C. 20007-5201

Library of Congress Cataloging-in-Publication Data

Takesuye, David.
   Urban Land Institute award winning projects 2005/David Takesuye; contributing author, Julie D. Stern.
      p. cm.
Includes bibliographical references and index.
ISBN-13: 978-0-87420-953-2 (alk. paper)
   1. Land use, Urban. I. Stern, Julie D. II. Urban Land Institute.
III. Title.
HD1391.T35 2005
333.77'13–dc22   2005028530

ISBN: 978-0-87420-953-2

10 9 8 7 6 5 4 3 2 1

Printed in the United States of America.

Design and composition
Marc Alain Meadows, Meadows Design Office Inc., Washington, D.C.
www.mdomedia.com

ULI–the Urban Land Institute is a nonprofit education and research institute that is supported by its members. Its mission is to provide responsible leadership in the use of land in order to enhance the total environment.

ULI sponsors education programs and forums to encourage an open international exchange of ideas and sharing of experiences; initiates research that anticipates emerging land use trends and issues and proposes creative solutions based on that research; provides advisory services; and publishes a wide variety of materials to disseminate information on land use and development. Established in 1936, the Institute today has more than 27,000 members from 80 countries, representing the entire spectrum of the land use and development disciplines. The Institute is recognized internationally as one of the industry's most respected and widely quoted sources of objective information on urban planning, growth, and development.

Project Staff

Rachelle L. Levitt
Executive Vice President, Policy and Practice
Publisher

Gayle Berens
Vice President, Real Estate Development Practice

David Takesuye
Senior Associate, Awards and Competition
Project Director

Nancy H. Stewart
Director, Book Program

Lori Hatcher
Director, Publications Marketing

Libby Howland
Manuscript Editor

David James Rose
Assistant Editor

Betsy VanBuskirk
Art Director

Karrie Underwood
Digital Images Assistant

Craig Chapman
Director, Publishing Operations

The ULI Awards for Excellence Program

A guiding principle of the Urban Land Institute is that the achievement of excellence in land use practice should be recognized and rewarded. For 26 years, ULI has honored outstanding development projects in both the private and public sectors with the ULI Awards for Excellence program, which today is widely recognized as the development community's most prestigious awards program. ULI Awards for Excellence recognize the full development process of a project, not just its architecture or design—although these elements play an important role in the overall project. Each award is presented to the development project, with the developer accepting on behalf of the project.

Nominations are open to all, not just ULI members. Finalists and winners are chosen by juries of ULI full members chaired by trustees. Jury members represent many fields of real estate development expertise, including finance, land planning, development, public affairs, design, and other professional services. They also represent a broad geographic diversity.

ULI began the Awards for Excellence program in 1979 with the objective of recognizing truly superior development efforts. The criteria for the awards involve factors that go beyond good design, including leadership, contribution to the community, innovations, public/private partnership, environmental protection and enhancement, response to societal needs, and financial success. Winning projects represent the highest standards of achievement in the development industry, standards that ULI members hold worthy of attainment in their professional endeavors. All types of projects have been recognized for their excellence, including office, residential, recreational, urban/mixed use, industrial/office park, commercial/retail, new community, rehabilitation, public, and heritage projects, as well as programs and projects that do not fit into any of these product categories.

For the first three years of the program, only one Award for Excellence was granted each year. In 1982, ULI trustees authorized awards for two winners—one large-scale project and one small-scale project—to recognize excellence regardless of size. Starting in 1985, the awards program shifted emphasis to product categories, while also retaining the small- and large-scale designations. As the program matured, new categories were added to reflect changes in the development industry. In 2002, the last year in which winners were awarded by category, there were 18 categories and up to 11 possible awards.

The Special Award was established in 1986 to acknowledge up to two projects and/or programs that are socially desirable but do not necessarily meet the official awards guidelines governing financial viability, and exemplary projects that are not easily categorized. In 1989, the Heritage Award was introduced to acknowledge projects that have established an industry standard for excellence, and that have been completed for at least 25 years. As of 2005, only six Heritage Awards have been granted.

When the awards program began, only projects located in the United States or Canada were considered. Beginning with the 1994 awards, ULI's board of trustees authorized the creation of an International Award for a project outside the United States and Canada. With the 2001 awards, the board eliminated this category, opening all categories to all projects, regardless of location.

In 2003, ULI eliminated all category designations, with the exception of the Heritage Award, and did more to recognize the excellence of all the finalist projects in the awards process, not just the award winners. In 2004, ULI inaugurated the ULI Awards for Excellence: Europe. Adopting the same criteria and a similar selection process, a six-person jury of Europe-based ULI members announced six winners from among 11 finalists, representing the best of 42 entries from 11 countries.

Now in its 27th year, the Awards for Excellence program continues to evolve with the introduction of the ULI Awards for Excellence: Asia Pacific. Building on the success of the Europe awards, the Asia Pacific awards program selected five winners in 2005. Also new in 2005 are the ULI Global Awards. A select jury of international trustees will choose up to five Global Award winners from among this year's 21 award-winning projects. The jury will announce these special winners at the Institute's 2005 Fall Meeting in Los Angeles, November 1–4, 2005.

The 2006 "Call for Entries" for the Americas, Europe, and Asia Pacific competitions are now available on the ULI Awards Web page (www.awards.uli.org).

Judging Criteria

1. Although architectural excellence is certainly a factor, the ULI Awards for Excellence is not a "beauty contest."

2. The project or program must be substantially completed. If the project is phased, the first phase must be completed and operationally stable.

3. No specific age or time constraints apply, except for the Heritage Award (which recognizes projects and/or programs that have been completed for at least 25 years).

4. The project must be financially viable, which means it must be in stable operation and financially successful. An applicant must be able to document

the prudent use of financial resources to justify the achievement of a financial return. Programs and projects developed by nonprofit or public agencies are necessarily exempt from the financial viability requirement.

5. The project must demonstrate relevance to the contemporary and future needs of the community in which it is located. The community reaction to the project also is taken into consideration.

6. The project must stand out from others in its category.

7. The project must be an exemplary representative of good development and a model for similar projects worldwide.

Selection Process

1. Applications are solicited via a "Call for Entries," available as a downloadable document on the ULI Web site's Awards page (www.awards.uli.org) on October 1.

2. Developers and/or other members of the development team submit completed applications to ULI by a given date in January. Each completed entry must contain the developer's name and signature.

3. The three Awards for Excellence juries—the Americas, Europe, and Asia Pacific—separately convene to review submissions and choose finalists.

4. Teams of two or three jury members visit each finalist project.

5. When all site visits have been completed, the respective juries reconvene to evaluate the finalist projects and choose award winners—up to ten in the Americas, five in Europe, and five in Asia Pacific. In the Americas, the jury may also choose one Heritage Award winner.

   The Americas awards are announced and officially honored at an awards ceremony at ULI's annual Spring Council Forum. The Europe and Asia Pacific awards are announced at their respective spring or summer conferences.

Past ULI Awards for Excellence Winners

The following 185 projects have received ULI Awards for Excellence. Each project name is followed by its location and its developer/owner.

1979 First year of award ▪ The Galleria; Houston, Texas; Hines Interests Limited Partnership

1980 Charles Center; Baltimore, Maryland; Baltimore City Development Corporation

1981 WDW/Reedy Creek; Orlando, Florida; The Walt Disney Company

1982 Two awards given: large- and small-scale ▪ Large-Scale: Heritage Village; Southbury, Connecticut; Heritage Development Group, Inc. ▪ Small-Scale: Promontory Point; Newport Beach, California; The Irvine Company

1983 Large-Scale: Eaton Centre; Toronto, Canada; Cadillac Fairview Limited

1984 Large-Scale: Embarcadero Center; San Francisco, California; Embarcadero Center, Ltd.; ▪ Small-Scale: Rainbow Centre; Niagara Falls, New York; The Cordish Company

1985 Introduction of product categories ▪ New Community: Las Colinas; Irving, Texas; JPI Partners, Inc. ▪ Large-Scale Residential: Museum Tower; New York, New York; The Charles H. Shaw Company ▪ Small-Scale Urban Mixed-Use: Sea Colony Condominiums; Santa Monica, California; Dominion Property Company ▪ Large-Scale Recreational: Sea Pines Plantation; Hilton Head, South Carolina; Community Development Institute ▪ Small-Scale Urban Mixed-Use: Vista Montoya; Los Angeles, California; Pico Union Neighborhood Council/Community Redevelopment Agency

1986 Introduction of rehabilitation and special categories ▪ Small-Scale Mixed-Use: 2000 Pennsylvania Avenue; Washington, D.C.; George Washington University ▪ Small-Scale Rehabilitation: Downtown Costa Mesa; Costa Mesa, California; PSB Realty Corporation ▪ Special: Inner Harbor Shoreline; Baltimore, Maryland; Baltimore City Development Corporation ▪ Large-Scale Recreational: Kaanapali Beach Resort; Kaanapali, Hawaii; Amfac/JMB Hawaii ▪ Large-Scale Residential: The Landings on Skidaway Island; Savannah, Georgia; The Bramigar Organization, Inc. ▪ Small-Scale Industrial/Office Park: The Purdue Frederick Company; Norwalk, Connecticut; The Purdue Frederick Company ▪ Large-Scale Recreational: Water Tower Place; Chicago, Illinois; JMB Realty Corporation

1987 Large-Scale Industrial/Office Park: Bishop Ranch Business Park; San Ramon, California; Sunset Development Company ▪ Small-Scale Commercial/Retail: Loews Ventana Canyon Resort; Tucson, Arizona; Estes Homebuilding ▪ Large-Scale Urban Mixed-Use: St. Louis Union Station; St. Louis, Missouri; The Rouse Company ▪ Small-Scale Residential: Straw Hill; Manchester, New Hampshire; George Matarazzo and Mark Stebbins ▪ Rehabilitation: The Willard Inter-Continental; Washington, D.C.; The Oliver Carr Company

1988 Large-Scale Urban Mixed-Use: Copley Place; Boston, Massachusetts; Urban Investment & Development Company ▪ Special: Downtown Women's Center; Los Angeles, California; The Ratkovitch Company ▪ Large-Scale Commercial/Retail: The Grand Avenue; Milwaukee, Wisconsin; Milwaukee Redevelopment Corporation (MRC) ▪ Rehabilitation: Northpoint; Chicago, Illinois; Amoco Neighborhood Development ▪ Small-Scale Residential: Pickleweed Apartments; Mill Valley, California; BRIDGE Housing Corporation ▪ Large-Scale Residential: Rector Place; New York, New York; Battery Park City Authority ▪ Small-Scale Office: Wilshire Palisades; Santa Monica, California; Tooley & Company

1989 Introduction of Heritage Award ▪ Small-Scale Urban Mixed-Use: Charleston Place; Charleston, South Carolina; The Taubman Company, Inc., and Cordish Embry Associates (joint venture) ▪ Rehabilitation: Commonwealth Development; Boston, Massachusetts; Corcoran Management ▪ Small-Scale Office: Escondido City Hall; Escondido, California; City of Escondido ▪ Large-Scale Office: Norwest Center; Minneapolis, Minnesota; Hines Interests ▪ Special: Pratt-Willert Neighborhood; Buffalo, New York; City of Buffalo ▪ New Community: Reston; Reston, Virginia; Mobil Land Development in Virginia ▪ Heritage: Rockefeller Center; New York, New York; The Rockefeller Group ▪ Large-Scale Urban Mixed-Use: Rowes Wharf; Boston, Massachusetts; The Beacon Companies

1990 Small-Scale Commercial: The Boulders; Carefree, Arizona; Westcor Partners ▪ Large-Scale Industrial: Carnegie Center; Princeton, New Jersey; Carnegie Center Associates ▪ Small-Scale Residential: Columbia Place; San Diego, California; Odmark & Thelan ▪ Large-Scale Residential: River Run; Boise, Idaho; O'Neill Enterprises, Inc. ▪ Special: Tent City; Boston, Massachusetts; Tent City Corporation ▪ Rehabilitation: Wayne County Building; Detroit, Michigan; Farbman Stein ▪ New Community: Woodlake; Richmond, Virginia; East West Partners of Virginia

1991 Small-Scale Commercial/Retail: Del Mar Plaza; Del Mar, California; Del Mar Partnership ▪ Large-Scale Urban Mixed-Use: Fashion Centre at Pentagon City; Arlington, Virginia; Melvin Simon & Associates, and Rose Associates ▪ Small-Scale Urban Mixed-Use: Garibaldi Square; Chicago, Illinois; The Charles H. Shaw Company ▪ Large-Scale Residential: Ghent Square; Norfolk, Virginia; Norfolk Redevelopment and Housing Authority ▪ Special: Grand Central Partnership; New York, New York; Grand Central Partnership ▪ Small-Scale Office: James R. Mills Building; San Diego, California; Starboard Development Corporation ▪ Rehabilitation: Marina Village; Alameda, California; Vintage Properties ▪ Special: Union Station; Washington, D.C.; Union Station Redevelopment Corporation

1992 Small-Scale Commercial/Retail: CocoWalk; Miami, Florida; Constructa U.S. ▪ Special: The Coeur d'Alene Resort Golf Course; Coeur d'Alene, Idaho; Hagadone Hospitality ▪ Special: The Delancey Street Foundation; San Francisco, California; The Delancey Street Foundation ▪ Public: Harbor Point; Boston, Massachusetts; Corcoran Jennison Companies ▪ Large-Scale Mixed-Use: Market Square; Washington, D.C.; Trammell Crow ▪ New Community: Planned Community of Mission Viejo; Mission Viejo, California; Mission Viejo Company ▪ Small-Scale Residential: Summit Place; St. Paul, Minnesota; Robert Engstrom Companies ▪ Rehabilitation: Tysons Corner Center; McLean, Virginia; The L&B Group

1993 Small-Scale Residential: Beverly Hills Senior Housing; Beverly Hills, California; Jewish Federation Council ▪ Special: Charlestown Navy Yard; Charlestown, Massachusetts; Boston Redevelopment Authority ▪ Heritage: The Country Club Plaza; Kansas City, Missouri; J.C. Nichols Company ▪ Large-Scale Residential: The Cypress of Hilton Head Island; Hilton Head Island, South Carolina; The Melrose Company ▪ Small-Scale Rehabilitation: Furness House; Baltimore, Maryland; The Cordish Company ▪ Large-Scale Recreational: Kapalua; Kapalua, Maui, Hawaii; Kapalua Land Company, Ltd. ▪ Special: Post Office Square Park and Garage; Boston, Massachusetts; Friends of Post Office Square, Inc. ▪ Rehabilitation: Schlitz Park; Mil-

waukee, Wisconsin; The Brewery Works, Inc. ▪ Small-Scale Commercial/Retail: The Somerset Collection; Troy, Michigan; Forbes/Cohen Properties and Frankel Associates

1994 Introduction of international category ▪ International: Broadgate; London, United Kingdom; Stanhope Properties ▪ Small-Scale Residential: Orchard Village; Chattanooga, Tennessee; Chattanooga Neighborhood Enterprise ▪ Public: Oriole Park at Camden Yards; Baltimore, Maryland; Maryland Stadium Authority ▪ Special: The Pennsylvania Avenue Plan; Washington, D.C.; Pennsylvania Avenue Development Corporation ▪ Large-Scale Rehabilitation: Phipps Plaza; Atlanta, Georgia; Compass Retail, Inc. ▪ Heritage: Sea Pines Plantation; Hilton Head Island, South Carolina; Charles Fraser ▪ Large-Scale Office: Washington Mutual Tower; Seattle, Washington; Wright Runstad and Company ▪ Large-Scale Residential: Woodbridge; Irvine, California; The Irvine Company ▪ Special: The Woodlands; The Woodlands, Texas; The Woodlands Corporation

1995 Small-Scale Rehabilitation: 640 Memorial Drive; Cambridge, Massachusetts; Massachusetts Institute of Technology Real Estate ▪ Large-Scale Commercial/Retail: Broadway Plaza; Walnut Creek, California; Macerich Northwestern Associates and The Macerich Company ▪ Heritage: Disneyland Park; Anaheim, California; The Walt Disney Company ▪ Large-Scale Industrial/Office: Irvine Spectrum; Orange County, California; The Irvine Company ▪ Small-Scale Recreational: Little Nell Hotel and Aspen Mountain Base; Aspen, Colorado; Aspen Skiing Company ▪ Special: Monterey Bay Aquarium; Monterey, California; The Monterey Bay Aquarium Foundation ▪ New Community: Pelican Bay; Naples, Florida; WCI Communities, LP ▪ Special: Riverbank State Park; New York, New York; New York State Office of Parks, Recreation and Historic Preservation ▪ Small-Scale Residential: Strathern Park Apartments; Sun Valley, California; Thomas Safran and Associates

1996 Large-Scale Residential: Avenel; Potomac, Maryland; Natelli Communities ▪ Public: Bryant Park; New York, New York; Bryant Park Restoration Corporation ▪ Large-Scale Office: Comerica Tower at Detroit Center; Detroit, Michigan; Hines Interests Limited Partnership ▪ Small-Scale Residential: The Court Home Collection at Valencia NorthPark; Valencia, California; The Newhall Land and Farming Company, and RGC ▪ Small-Scale Commercial/Hotel: The Forum Shops; Las Vegas, Nevada; Simon Property Group ▪ Small-Scale Mixed-Use: The Heritage on the Garden; Boston, Massachusetts; The Druker Company ▪ Large-Scale Recreational: Kiawah Island; Kiawah Island, South Carolina; Kiawah Resort Associates LP ▪ Special: The Scattered Site Program; Chicago, Illinois; The Habitat Company

1997 Heritage: The Arizona Biltmore Hotel and Resort; Phoenix, Arizona; Grossman Company Properties ▪ Rehabilitation: Chelsea Piers; New York, New York; Chelsea Piers, LP ▪ Large-Scale Recreational: Desert Mountain; Scottsdale, Arizona; Desert Mountain Properties ▪ Rehabilitation: Eagles Building Restoration; Seattle, Washington; A Contemporary Theater and Housing Resources Group (general partners) ▪ Small-Scale Residential: Mercado Apartments; San Diego, California; City of San Diego Redevelopment Agency ▪ Large-Scale Commercial/Hotel: Park Meadows; Park Meadows, Colorado; TrizecHahn Centers ▪ Special: Pennsylvania Convention Center; Philadelphia, Pennsylvania; Pennsylvania Convention Center Authority ▪ Special: A Safe House for Kids and Moms; Irvine, California; Human Options ▪ Public: Smyrna Town Center; Smyrna, Georgia; City of Smyrna, Knight-Davidson Companies (residential) and Thomas Enterprises (retail/offices) ▪ International: Stockley Park at Heathrow; Uxbridge, Middlesex, United Kingdom; Stanhope Properties, PLC

1998 Large-Scale Business Park: Alliance; Fort Worth, Texas; Hillwood Development Corporation ▪ Special: American Visionary Art Museum; Baltimore, Maryland; Rebecca and LeRoy E. Hoffberger ▪ International: Calakmul; Mexico City, Mexico; Francisco G. Coronado (owner) ▪ Small-Scale Residential: Courthouse Hill; Arlington, Virginia; Eakin/Youngentob Associates, Inc. ▪ Public: Harold Washington Library Center; Chicago, Illinois; U.S. Equities Realty (developer) ▪ Special: Richmond City Center; Richmond, California; BRIDGE Housing Corporation (owner) ▪ Rehabilitation: Twenty-Eight State Street; Boston, Massachusetts; Equity Office Properties Trust ▪ Rehabilitation: UtiliCorp United World Headquarters/New York Life Building; Kansas City, Missouri; The Zimmer Companies ▪ Small-Scale Recreational: Village Center; Beaver Creek, Colorado; East West Partners

1999 Small-Scale Rehabilitation: Bayou Place; Houston, Texas; The Cordish Company ▪ Large-Scale Residential: Bonita Bay; Bonita Springs, Florida; Bonita Bay Properties, Inc. ▪ Public: Chicago Public Schools Capital Improvement Program; Chicago, Illinois; Chicago Public Schools ▪ Small-Scale Commercial/Hotel: The Commons at Calabasas; Calabasas, California; Caruso Affiliated Holdings ▪ Special: Coors Field; Denver, Colorado; Denver Metropolitan Stadium District ▪ Small-Scale Mixed-Use: East Pointe; Milwaukee, Wisconsin; Milwaukee Redevelopment Corporation and Mandel Group, Inc. ▪ Large-Scale Recreational: Hualalai; Ka'upulehu-Kona, Hawaii; Ka'upulehu Makai Venture/Hualalai Development Company ▪ Large-Scale Rehabilitation: John Hancock Center; Chicago, Illinois; U.S. Equities Realty ▪ Small-Scale Residential: Normandie Village; Los Angeles, California; O.N.E. Company, SIPA ▪ Small-Scale Commercial/Hotel: Seventh & Collins Parking Facility (Ballet Valet); Miami Beach, Florida; City of Miami Beach, Goldman Properties ▪ International: Vinohradský Pavilon; Prague, Czech Republic; Prague Investment, a.s.

2000 Small-Scale Rehabilitation: Amazon.com Building; Seattle, Washington; Wright Runstad and Company ▪ Heritage: The Burnham Plan; Chicago, Illinois; The Commercial Club of Chicago ▪ Small-Scale Residential: The Colony; Newport Beach, California; Irvine Apartment Communities ▪ Large-Scale Residential: Coto de Caza; Orange County, California; Lennar Communities ▪ Small-Scale Mixed-Use: DePaul Center; Chicago, Illinois; DePaul University ▪ Public: NorthLake Park Community School; Orlando, Florida; Lake Nona Land Company ▪ Large-Scale Rehabilitation: The Power Plant; Baltimore, Maryland; The Cordish Company ▪ International: Sony Center am Potsdamer Platz; Berlin, Germany; Tishman Speyer Properties, Sony Corporation, Kajima Corporation, and BE-ST Development GmbH & Co. (owner) ▪ Special: Spring Island; Beaufort County, South Carolina; Chaffin/Light Associates ▪ Public: The Townhomes on Capitol Hill; Washington, D.C.; Ellen Wilson CDC and Telesis Corporation ▪ Large-Scale Recreational: Whistler Village/Blackcomb Benchlands; Whistler, British Columbia, Canada; Resort Municipality of Whistler, and INTRAWEST Corporation

2001 International category eliminated ▪ New Community: Celebration; Celebration, Florida; The Celebration Company ▪ Special: Dewees Island; Dewees Island, South Carolina; Island Preservation Partnership ▪ Large-Scale Residential: Harbor Steps; Seattle, Washington; Harbor Properties, Inc. ▪ Small-Scale Rehabilitation; Pier 1; San Francisco, California; AMB Property Corporation ▪ Small-Scale Recreational: The Reserve; Indian Wells, California; Lowe Enterprises, Inc. ▪ Small-Scale Office: Thames Court; London, United Kingdom; Markborough Properties Limited ▪ Special: Townhomes at Oxon Creek; Washington, D.C.; William C. Smith & Company, Inc. ▪ Large-Scale Mixed-Use: Valencia Town Center Drive; Valencia, California;

The Newhall Land and Farming Company ▪ Large-Scale Commercial/Hotel: The Venetian Casino Resort; Las Vegas, Nevada; LVS/Development Group ▪ Public: Yerba Buena Gardens; San Francisco, California; Yerba Buena Alliance

2002 Small-Scale Mixed-Use: Bethesda Row; Bethesda, Maryland; Federal Realty Investment Trust ▪ Large-Scale Mixed-Use: CityPlace; West Palm Beach, Florida; The Related Companies ▪ Special: Envision Utah; Salt Lake City, Utah; Coalition for Utah's Future ▪ Public: Homan Square Community Center Campus; Chicago, Illinois; Homan Square Community Center Foundation (owner) and The Shaw Company (developer) ▪ Small-Scale Rehabilitation: Hotel Burnham at the Reliance Building; Chicago, Illinois; McCaffery Interests ▪ Special: Memphis Ballpark District; Memphis, Tennessee; Memphis Redbirds Foundation (owner), and Parkway Properties, Inc. (developer) ▪ Large-Scale Office: One Raffles Link; Singapore Central, Singapore; Hongkong Land Property Co., Ltd. ▪ Small-Scale Rehabilitation: REI Denver Flagship Store; Denver, Colorado; Recreational Equipment, Inc. ▪ Large-Scale Recreational: Station Mont Tremblant; Quebec, Canada; Intrawest ▪ New Community: Summerlin North; Las Vegas, Nevada; The Rouse Company

2003 Product categories eliminated ▪ Atago Green Hills; Tokyo, Japan; Mori Building Company ▪ Ayala Center Greenbelt 3; Makati City, Manila, Philippines; Ayala Land, Inc. ▪ Bay Harbor; Bay Harbor, Michigan; Victor International Corporation ▪ Chattahoochee River Greenway; Georgia; Chattahoochee River Coordinating Committee ▪ The Grove and Farmers Market; Los Angeles, California; Caruso Affiliated Holdings (The Grove), and A.F. Gilmore Company (Farmers Market) ▪ Millennium Place; Boston, Massachusetts; Millennium Partners/MDA Associates ▪ Shanghai Xintiandi (North Block); Shanghai, China; Shui On Group ▪ The Town of Seaside; Seaside, Florida; Seaside Community Development Corporation ▪ The Villages of East Lake; Atlanta, Georgia; East Lake Community Foundation, Inc. ▪ The West Philadelphia Initiatives; Philadelphia, Pennsylvania; University of Pennsylvania

2004 The Americas and Asia Pacific: Baldwin Park; Orlando, Florida; Baldwin Park Development Company ▪ Fall Creek Place; Indianapolis, Indiana; City of Indiana (owner), Mansur Real Estate Services, Inc., and King Park Area Development Corporation (developers) ▪ First Ward Place/The Garden District; Charlotte, North Carolina; City of Charlotte (owner), Banc of America Community Development Corporation (master developer) ▪ The Fullerton Square Project; Singapore; Far East Organization/Sino Land ▪ Playhouse Square Center; Cleveland, Ohio; Playhouse Square Foundation ▪ The Plaza at PPL Center; Allentown, Pennsylvania; Liberty Property Trust ▪ Technology Square at Georgia Institute of Technology; Atlanta, Georgia; Georgia Institute of Technology and Georgia Tech Foundation (owners), Jones Lang LaSalle (development manager) ▪ University Park at MIT; Cambridge, Massachusetts; Forest City Enterprises, City of Cambridge Community Development Department, and Massachusetts Institute of Technology ▪ Walt Disney Concert Hall; Los Angeles, California; Los Angeles County (owner), Walt Disney Concert Hall, Inc. (developer) ▪ WaterColor; Seagrove Beach, Florida; The St. Joe Company

2004 Europe: Brindleyplace; Birmingham, United Kingdom; Argent Group, PLC ▪ Bullring; Birmingham, United Kingdom; The Birmingham Alliance ▪ Casa de les Punxes; Barcelona, Spain; Inmobiliaria Colonial ▪ Diagonal Mar; Barcelona, Spain; Hines Interests España ▪ Promenaden Hauptbahnhof Leipzig; Leipzig, Germany; ECE Projektmanagement GmbH & Co., Deutsche Bahn AG, and DB Immobilienfonds ▪ Regenboogpark; Tilburg, The Netherlands; AM Wonen

CONTENTS

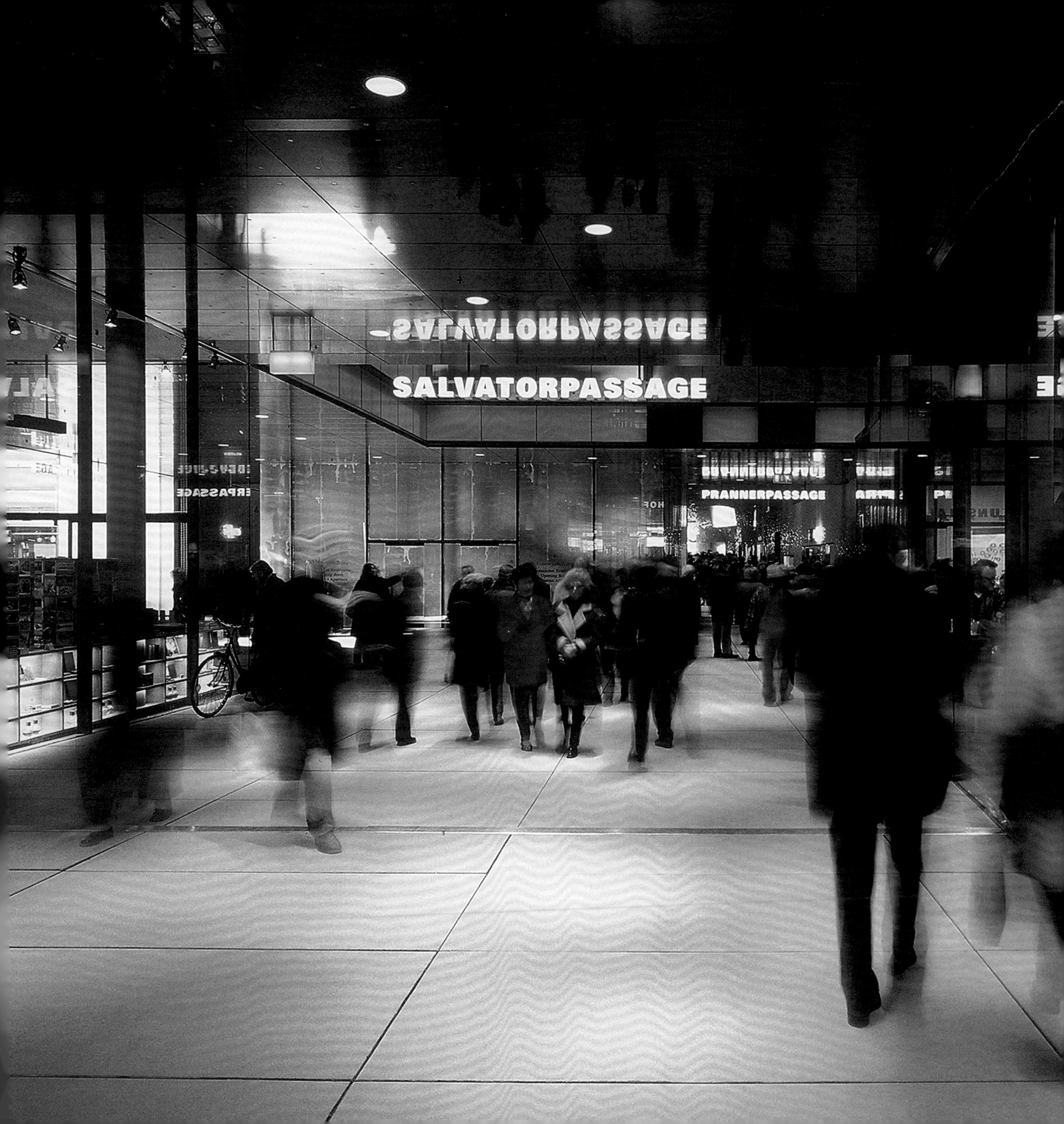

SALVATORPASSAGE
PRANNERPASSAGE

COMMERCIAL

ARKADIA SHOPPING CENTER

Warsaw, Poland

Development Team

Owner/Developer

ERE-Groupe BEG
Paris, France
www.groupebeg.com

Architects

RTKL (design architect)
Baltimore, Maryland
www.rtkl.com

Biuro Projektowe Nyczak
(architect of record)
Warsaw, Poland

BEG Ingénierie (executive architect)
Orleans, France
www.beg-ing.com

Arkadia is a major new 109,348-square-meter (1.18 million sf) retail/entertainment complex on the northern edge of downtown Warsaw. Its main entry plaza marks the site of the former train station from which Jews in the nearby Warsaw ghetto were transported to extermination camps.

In concept, the development is based on the European tradition of "trade passages"—art nouveau era shopping arcades featuring glass roofs over markets and stalls. Baltimore-based architecture firm RTKL created four such arcades, each with a theme relating to Polish history. Three levels of retail sit atop two levels of parking. The retail component includes a Carrefour hypermarket and a Leroy-Merlin do-it-yourself store, as well as 230 shops, 15 restaurants, a food court with ten vendors, and a 15-screen cinema.

It was the great forces of history that made this site available for development at this time. Ever since the country overthrew the Communist Party in 1989, Poland has been determined to join the market economies of Europe—obtaining, for example, membership in the North Atlantic Treaty Organization (NATO) in 1999 and the European Union (EU) in 2003. Poland's new orientation to Europe has had cascading effects on Polish lifestyles. The 1994 referendum that initiated Poland's membership in the EU required the privatization of state-owned railroads. This triggered a repurposing of railroad assets, an undertaking involving thousands of discrete operations and real properties. By 2001, PKP, the Polish national railroad company, finally was able to privatize the nine-hectare (22 ac) warehousing and railyard parcel where Arkadia was eventually developed.

European Retail Enterprise (ERE) saw an opportunity in this brownfield site, even though it was located in a city (and country) with only a recent history of economic growth and was isolated from the commercial heart of the city by a divided highway and railroad tracks. Nevertheless, the highway and the rail tracks connected the site to the city. And the site was only ten minutes from the city center and its potential customer base of 172,000 people. More than 500,000 people live within 15 minutes of the site and 1 million live within a 30-minute radius. Still, with three other shopping malls in the planning stages for elsewhere in Warsaw and with Poland still marked as a former Eastern European country, even in 2001, the development team's commitment to this project required a leap of faith.

Since it opened in October 2004 in a highly competitive market, 1.5 million people a month have visited Arkadia, which is open seven days a week and is 98 percent leased. As EU members, Poles expect a diverse array of goods and services. At Arkadia they can find them.

COMMERCIAL · FINALIST

Project Data

Web Site www.arkadia.com.pl

Site Area 9 hectares (22 ac)

Facilities

302,207 square meters (3.25 million sf) gross building area

109,348 square meters (1.18 million sf) gross leasable retail space

15,000 square meters (161,460 sf) public open space and interior plazas

4,030 structured parking spaces

Land Uses retail, entertainment, public plaza, parking

Completion Date October 2004

BERGOGNONE 53

Milan, Italy

Development Team

Owner/Developer

Hines Italia, Srl.
Milan, Italy
www.hines.com

Architect

MCA Integrated Design, Srl.
Bologna, Italy
www.mcarchitects.it

Project Data

Site Area **0.5 hectare (1.26 ac)**

Facilities

22,000 square meters (236,800 sf)
total building area

14,500 square meters (156,082 sf)
leasable office space

2,000 square meters (21,529 sf)
leasable retail space

100 parking spaces

Land Uses

office, retail/restaurant, open space
(courtyards), parking

Completion Date

December 2004

Named after its address in Milan's Porta Genova neighborhood, Bergognone 53 is a refurbishment of four nondescript buildings, in effect turning them into an important landmark in the rejuvenating neighborhood. A marquee tenant was secured, setting off an influx of fashion, media, and advertising studios that has branded Porta Genova as a fashionable neighborhood. Environmentally friendly mechanical systems were installed, which reinforced the project's with-it image while qualifying it for tax breaks.

Porta Genova is a well-located neighborhood—close to downtown and to the nightlife found in the Navigli district and served well by transportation, including the ring road around Milan and other highways, subways, and its own train station (Porta Genova). In 2000, however, it was characterized by obsolete industrial buildings, many of them abandoned. After conducting a thorough market analysis Hines bought four of these buildings—from the Italian postal service, which once had had its regional headquarters there—in a bidding process that started at €110 million ($103 million).

These were not historic buildings and it would have been easier and cheaper to tear them down than to renovate them. But building regulations prohibited the addition of new floor space and there were no design precedents in Porta Genova for new construction. Hines decided that refurbishment would be more in keeping with the character of the neighborhood.

An international architectural competition among 11 firms was won by Mario Cucinella Architects (MCA Integrated Design) with a design that called for a glass canopy to cover the 900 square meters (9,688 sf) of open space between the four buildings, thus linking them visually and functionally. The steel and glass in the canopy and the bright colors of the exterior walls relate to the original industrial design of these and nearby buildings. Photovoltaic cells on the roof of one of the buildings add another industrial flourish and generate electricity for common area lighting, earning Hines a grant of €87,000 ($107,000) from the regional Lombardian government.

Having pursued international credit tenants from the start, Hines landed Deloitte while the project was still under construction. To serve a potential population of 1,600 workers within Bergognone 53 as well as other people in Porta Genova, the developer incorporated a number of amenities, including a daycare center, two restaurants, and underground parking for 100 cars. The four-building complex could be easily partitioned for four or more tenants, but Deloitte remains the sole tenant.

Since the project's completion in 2004, Porta Genova has experienced the conversion of a number of industrial buildings to mixed use. With Giorgio Armani moving its headquarters studio (designed by Tadao Ando) next door to Bergognone 53, Porta Genova—thanks in large part to the highly visible Bergognone 53—is gathering momentum as Milan's new hip neighborhood.

RUE PAUL CEZANNE

CÉZANNE SAINT-HONORÉ

Paris, France

Paris's eighth arrondissement, the traditional business district surrounding the Champs-Elysées, remains a low-rise district that Georges-Eugène Haussmann—Napoleon III's city planner who designed and executed the grand baroque boulevards that make Paris a preeminent European city—would recognize. The medieval streets that run behind and between the boulevards make Paris a French city. And rue Paul Cézanne is an archetypically French street that is only 15 meters (49 ft) wide from building face to building face and 100 meters (328 ft) long.

Twin 1930s art nouveau office buildings—connected by arcaded passageways under the street—occupy both sides of the block. The passageways were being used for parking, while uncontrolled surface parking at the point where the street should have emptied onto rue de Courcelles obstructed vehicular

Development Team

Owners/Developers

Société Foncière Lyonnaise
Paris, France
www.fonciere-lyonnaise.com

Predica
Paris, France
www.ca-predica.fr

Architect

Braun & Associes
Paris, France
www.f-s-braun.fr

and pedestrian access to rue Paul Cézanne. A state agency had occupied the buildings since the 1950s. In 2001, two developers, Société Foncière Lyonnaise and Predica, purchased the property for €105.6 million ($132 million). The developers planned to refurbish the functionally obsolete, poorly maintained, and half empty property to take advantage of its prime office market location.

Their first and most far-reaching step was to open rue Paul Cézanne at both ends to create a block-long pedestrianway. To make the street inviting and return it to full public use, the original macadam paving was replaced with new brick, and planters, trees, and benches were installed. The jumble of surface and underground parking was consolidated with underground parking for 127 cars. The subterranean connection between the two buildings was recovered for use, which added 5,000 square meters (53,820 sf) of usable space. A central rotunda in the under-the-street connector was fitted with a domed skylight that projects above the street and brings daylight to an area that has been converted to a staff lunchroom and conference rooms.

The two eight-story buildings yielded 28,420 square meters (305,900 sf) of office space and 1,355 square meters (14,585 sf) of retail space. Many fine, 1930s period details—such as stair rails, balconies, and carved exterior limestone facades—were restored. At the same time, the interior spaces were redesigned with flexible layouts catering to the evolving Parisian business culture. Because the number of internal load-bearing walls was limited, it was possible to design large, open office work areas.

Cézanne Saint-Honoré is a resounding economic success. The first phase, which was completed in May 2004, is fully leased and occupied, with rents at the top of the current market and revenue yields significantly above average for the Paris office market. The complex can compete for most of the potential tenants that desire an eighth arrondissement address. Completed in March 2005, Phase 2 was almost fully leased before its completion.

In summary, two underused buildings on an unknown street have been transformed into a readily identifiable office landmark in the heart of Paris's best-known business neighborhood. Cézanne Saint-Honoré—including the reclaimed street that it straddles—is a thriving part of the city. By restoring the buildings and the street, the developers of Cézanne Saint-Honoré restored a neighborhood.

Project Data

Site Area 4,190 square meters (45,102 sf)

Facilities

29,775 square meters (320,500 sf) total area

28,420 square meters (305,900 sf) leasable office space

1,355 square meters (14,585 sf) leasable retail space

127 parking spaces

Land Uses

office, public street, parking

Completion Dates

May 2004 for Phase 1

March 2005 for Phase 2

Jury Statement

Rue Paul Cézanne was an underused cul-de-sac in Paris's business district until the developers of Cézanne Saint-Honoré rescued an under-the-street connector between facing historic buildings. This allowed the street to be redeveloped as a tree-lined pedestrianway and opened the interior of the block to through traffic. The formerly obsolete buildings have returned 28,420 square meters (305,900 sf) of prime office space to the market and the developers have refitted a superbly preserved piece of traditional architecture to modern standards.

CHESTERFIELD SQUARE

Los Angeles, California

Development Team

Owners/Developers

Katell Properties, LLC
Long Beach, California
www.katellproperties.com

Capital Visions Equities
Los Angeles, California

Architect and Site Planner

Nadel Architects, Inc.
Los Angeles, California
www.nadelarc.com

Project Data

Site Area **22.4 acres (9 ha)**

Facilities

250,000 square feet (23,226 m²)
total building area

83,000 square feet (7,711 m²)
landscaped open space

1,283 parking spaces

Land Use **retail**

Completion Date **August 2004**

For a decade following Los Angeles's civil unrest in 1992, the South Central neighborhood was in a downward spiral of economic disinvestment, loss of pride, and loss of hope. Chesterfield Square, an infill community shopping center, was the first meaningful development project to occur in South Central in over a decade. While offering the community a commercial anchor and a point from which to finally rebuild, it also has yielded financial returns for its investors.

"If I didn't think this was going to make money, I wouldn't have done it," says lead developer Gerald Katell, who was motivated by a 1999 report from Pepperdine University that pointed to a strong consumer market: The residents of South Central were spending $900 million a year outside their neighborhood, the average household income was $37,000 (35 percent higher than the census and tax records), and 500,000 people lived within a three-mile radius of South Central. Many houses in the neighborhood were still well maintained, but the commercial corridors—dominated by barred windows, chain-link fences, and spray-painted graffiti—presented another picture.

Christopher W. Hammond, CEO of Capital Visions Equities and this project's codeveloper, had put down a $100,000 deposit on an 11-acre (4.45 ha) industrial site planned for subsidized residential development. The site's location near a major intersection (Western and Slauson avenues) prompted Katell and Hammond to consider a community retail development, which would require significant additional acreage. The developers had the strong support of the community in assembling the remainder of the site.

Katell personally guaranteed a 90 percent land loan at a blended interest rate of 19 percent. Home Depot's purchase of a pad site triggered a construction loan and mezzanine financing from Bank of America. Home Depot's commitment to an anchor position of 132,000 square feet (12,263 m²) encouraged Food 4 Less to lease 60,000 square feet (5,574 m²). When the property was 93 percent leased, the developers closed a 7.16 percent permanent loan with Nationwide Life Insurance, which they recently retired with a new loan from Greenwich Capital at 5.57 percent.

Walgreen's, at 17,125 square feet (1,591 m²), is the third major tenant. One-quarter of the 17 smaller tenants are local chains or locally owned. The median size of the smaller stores is 1,508 square feet (149 m²).

The design of Chesterfield Square is relatively simple—a happy coincidence of what the neighbors wanted and what could be afforded for the project to pencil out. The developers and neighbors were adamant about not wanting the type of iron fences and concertina wire that isolate strip centers in this neighbor-

hood, so five-foot-high (1.5 m) grassy berms surround the center's three street sides. Other ameliorating touches in this project are generous landscaped areas and top-of-the-line tenant fixtures and furnishings.

Almost 600 new jobs have been created at Chesterfield Square, 60 percent of which are held by neighborhood residents. With strong sales that make Chesterfield Square's tenants top performers in their respective chains, tenants pay rents that are nearly as high as those on the west side of Los Angeles. The Food 4 Less is one of the top producers in that chain, the Radio Shack store is one of the top three Radio Shack locations in the state, and the Home Depot is grossing more than the projected estimates. "This project was a win-win for all involved—the community, the retailers that saw the potential, the city of Los Angeles, the construction and permanent lenders, and the developers," says Katell, adding that Chesterfield Square "is the project of which I am most proud in my 41 years of development and it points the way for others who may now take a chance on inner-city development."

Project Data

Web Site www.fuenfhoefe.de

Site Area 1.4 hectares (3.5 ac)

Facilities

78,000 square meters (839,612 sf)
total building area

48,140 square meters (518,192 sf)
total leasable area

26,000 square meters (279,871 sf)
leasable office space

16,000 square meters (172,228 sf)
leasable retail space

3,140 square meters (33,800 sf)
residential space; 27 apartments

3,000 square meters (32,293 sf)
art gallery/exhibition area

220 parking spaces

Land Uses retail, office,
residential, art gallery

Completion Date March 2003

CITYQUARTIER FÜNF HÖFE

Munich, Germany

Situated in a 19th-century banking district in the heart of historic Munich, CityQuartier Fünf Höfe, a lifestyle center, is a complex of buildings featuring five courtyards ("fünf Höfe" in German) surrounded by shops and restaurants. Office space and apartments occupy the upper stories. The developer's reconfiguration of an entire block opened up this important urban site for shopping, eating, and relaxing—after many years of public inaccessibility.

In 1998, almost all the buildings on the block came under single ownership, and between 1999 and 2003, the block was completely reconfigured according to a design by Jacques Herzog and Pierre de Meuron, 2001 Pritzker Architecture Prize laureates. The goal was to create a pedestrian-friendly shopping environment with urban amenities, such as cafés and cultural attractions. By consolidating the spaces between buildings and in the middle of the block, the architects created five courtyards, each with walkways to the street, surrounded with shops and dining establishments. Hanging plants and artworks produce a sophisticated ambience within each courtyard. The artworks include a massive suspended stainless-steel sphere by Olafur Eliasson, colored wall designs by Rémy Zaugg, and photographic prints displayed on concrete floor panels by Thomas Ruff. A second-story art gallery is a major cultural attraction.

The retail space is fully leased to an attractive mix of 54 upscale tenants, including Armani and Ludwig Beck. An on-site management team offers comprehensive services and can respond rapidly to tenants' needs. Fünf Höfe was purchased by DIFA Deutsche Immobilien Fonds, AG, after it was completed, and it is one of several developments that DIFA markets under the CityQuartier product brand—the underlying philosophy of which is that places to live and places to work need not be separate places. The project's residential component is also fully leased, and the office component is at 95 percent occupancy.

Noting that the Fünf Höfe complex enjoys an outstanding central location close to the city hall, the Frauenkirche (Cathedral Church of Our Lady), the national theater, and the Bayerischer Hof hotel, Susanne Kaschub, head of marketing communications for DIFA, explains that "CityQuartier Fünf Höfe is part of a specific product line developed by DIFA that focuses strongly on meeting people's needs and enhancing the appeal of the urban center through a mix of uses. The Fünf Höfe complex makes an excellent fit with DIFA's investment strategy, which focuses on cohesive developments in central locations that combine a range of uses."

Development Team

Owner

DIFA Deutsche Immobilien Fonds, AG
Hamburg, Germany
www.difa.de

Developers

Fünf Höfe GmbH & Co., KG
Munich, Germany

HVB Immobilien, AG
Munich, Germany
www.hvbimmobilien.de

Architects

Herzog & de Meuron
Basel, Switzerland

Hilmer & Sattler
Munich, Germany

COMMERCIAL · WINNER

DANUBE HOUSE

Prague, Czech Republic

Close to the center of Prague and on the Vltava River, Danube House is beginning to transform a 66-hectare (163 ac) brownfield site that was occupied by railway yards and storage sheds into a pedestrian-oriented, mixed-use district comprising offices, hotels, housing, shops, and restaurants. The overall business park development is known as River City. Danube House is the first building to be developed in River City, and it serves as a landmark and gateway from Prague.

Danube House is an office/retail structure in the shape of a wedge that rises to 11 stories on its western prow. Its street-facing southern edge features a glazed atrium that acts as a noise buffer. Walkways and stairs along the outer atrium wall provide views of historic Prague. The exterior design reflects a respect for Czech traditions with its use of red sandstone and glass. The development includes a footbridge that crosses over a busy street to provide pedestrian access to the riverfront.

Danube House's inclusion of a wide range of innovative sustainable energy elements is a first for buildings in central Europe. Fresh air from the riverbank is brought into the building through underground concrete culverts that also cool the air. External sunshades on south- and east-facing windows reduce heat gain in the summer. Windows can be opened to provide natural ventilation during temperate spring and autumn days and summer nights. Mechanisms like these have resulted in operating costs that are two-thirds of those in comparable buildings.

The building features many handmade details that enrich the quality of the building. These would have been prohibitively expensive in a typical U.S. or western European construction project, but were affordable here because of the high level of craftsmanship extant in the Czech Republic. The prohibitive expense of importing many products that are standard components in office buildings in western Europe or the United States, on the other hand, challenged the design team, and it ended up that a number of components were designed locally and fabricated on site.

In August 2002, less than half a year before the planned opening of the building, an unexpected catastrophe in the form of a 500-year flood occurred, and the opening was delayed for (only) a few months. Danube House opened in July 2003, and it has since become home to a variety of Czech companies with international shareholders.

"Danube House was planned as the flagship building for the River City Prague development," says Petr Urbánek, managing director of Europolis Real Estate Asset Management. Explaining that the 1997 brief for the River City development called for buildings that harmonize with the existing urban environment; development on a human scale; buildings that in spirit display friendliness, structure, and identification; and low operating costs, Urbánek goes on to say that Danube House's "realization of this

Development Team

Owner/Developer

Europolis Real Estate Asset Management, s.r.o.
Prague, Czech Republic
www.europolis.cz

Architects

Kohn Pedersen Fox Associates (International), PA
London, United Kingdom
www.kpf.com

RFR
Paris, France
www.rfr.fr

A.D.N.S., s.r.o.
Prague, Czech Republic
www.adns.cz

Project Manager

Homola AYH, s.r.o.
Prague, Czech Republic
www.homola.de

Landscape Designer

Artflora
Olomouc, Czech Republic
www.artflora.cz

Project Data

Web Sites

www.danubehouse.cz

www.rivercity.cz

Site Area

1.15 hectares (2.8 ac)

Facilities

25,000 square meters (269,100 sf) total area

19,800 square meters (213,125 sf) leasable office space

1,200 square meters (12,920 sf) leasable retail space

253 parking spaces

Land Uses office, retail, parking

Completion Date July 2003

Jury Statement

On the banks of the Vltava River east of the ancient center of Prague, on a site formerly occupied by railway yards and warehouses, Danube House's 19,800 square meters (213,125 sf) of office space and 1,200 square meters (12,920 sf) of retail space have begun to transform a brownfield site. The wedge-shaped building of red sandstone and glass incorporates innovative energy-saving features that have helped establish a new benchmark for reduced operating costs. Danube House also establishes a landmark entry to the emerging River City mixed-use district.

concept by the use of environmentally sustainable technology and international architecture; the fact that the project is part of an urban development on a unique, regenerated site; and its market acceptance and current recognition by the professional community have confirmed—100 percent—the success of the original plan, despite a devastating flood just a few months before the scheduled completion."

The building's available office space is 85 percent leased, which exceeds local market conditions. Based on this success, Europolis completed in summer 2005 a second River City project, Nile House, which includes 17,900 square meters (192,675 sf) of office space and 1,100 square meters (11,840 sf) of retail space.

GOVERNMENT OFFICES GREAT GEORGE STREET

London, United Kingdom

The refurbishment of Government Offices Great George Street (GOGGS) is at once a flagship case study of a successful private finance initiative (PFI)—a U.K. program put into effect to transfer the development risks for government projects from the public to the private sector—and also a high-quality renovation project that treats government property and employees with the same care as a developer would treat private sector owners or tenants.

GOGGS is a Grade II–listed building in the heart of Whitehall, opposite the houses of Parliament and Westminster Abbey. Originally completed in 1917, it has been since 1945 the main office of Her Majesty's Treasury (HMT), which is headed by the chancellor of the exchequer. Designed for an earlier age, GOGGS was determined to be inadequate for today's civil service and its renovation was put out for bid as a PFI project. In 1996, Exchequer Partnership (EP) was selected as the developer.

Under the PFI program, developers bid on the project and the winning team assumes all development and operational responsibility for a negotiated term in exchange for collecting a fixed annual payment. For this project, EP negotiated an annual rent of £14.1 million (€22 million/$21 million) for Phase 1 and £17.1 million (€25.7 million/$31 million) for Phase 2 for terms of 35 and 33 years, respectively. The GOGGS PFI was the first such HMT project for which a standard terms and conditions contract was negotiated. The contract stipulated a schedule of fees and payments for certain cost-related occurrences. The GOGGS project was also the first PFI project for which a government/developer team conducted a funding competition among potential lenders for the right to finance the development, a process that saved £13 million (€19.5 million/$23.6 million) over the life of the concession.

Under the PFI, EP would be responsible for maintaining GOGGS for 35 years according to agreed standards. This long term encourages EP to act as an owner would act under the same circumstances. For example, knowing that it is responsible for the building's maintenance over the term, EP is likely to consider durability an important factor in specifying materials and architectural elements. For the project, this has resulted in predictably higher initial development costs and lower operational costs. Other conditions in the negotiated contract included a provision that the HMT staff would not have to vacate the premises during the building's refurbishment and a provision that EP would be responsible for obtaining any necessary permits. The PFI arrangements allowed the government to transfer key risks—such as latent defects—to the developer, and to outsource the management of a depreciating asset.

Development Team

Owners

Her Majesty's Treasury
London, United Kingdom
www.hm-treasury.gov.uk

Her Majesty's Revenue and Customs
London, United Kingdom
www.hmrc.gov.uk

Private Finance Consortium

Exchequer Partnership (Stanhope; and Bovis Lend Lease)
London, United Kingdom

Development Manager

Stanhope, PLC
London, United Kingdom
www.stanhopeplc.com

Construction Manager

Bovis Lend Lease
London, United Kingdom
www.bovislendlease.com

Architects

Foster & Partners
London, United Kingdom
www.fosterandpartners.com

Feilden & Mawson
London, United Kingdom
www.feildenandmawson.com

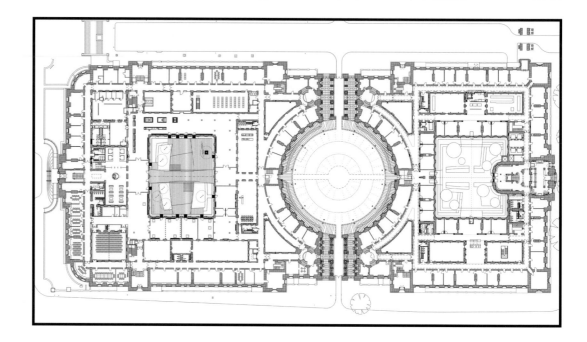

Project Data

Site Area **2 hectares (5 ac)**

Facilities

93,903 square meters (1 million sf) total leasable area

Land Uses **office**

Completion Dates

July 2002 for Phase 1

November 2004 for Phase 2

Jury Statement

The public/private refurbishment of a Grade II–listed property opposite the houses of Parliament reintegrates the Victorian era building with its Westminster neighborhood. All 93,903 square meters (1 million sf) of office space has been leased back to the government, and the refurbishment of Government Offices Great George Street has emerged as a new model for the development of worker-friendly government office buildings with outstanding design and amenities.

The renovation included the elimination of many corridors (representing 27 kilometers, or 17 miles, of walls), light wells, staircases, and other unproductive space and the redesign of the work areas as flexible, modern, efficient office space providing an open and collaborative working environment. The amount of usable space was increased by 25 percent and the number of HMT employees/contractors accommodated by the building rose from 850 to 1,200 in Phase 1 and to 3,100 in Phase 2. Other measures taken include the replacement of all 3,150 windows and all doors; the updating of mechanical, electrical, and telecommunications services; and the installation of artworks throughout the building.

EP delivered its brief. Because of the smooth development process, the government is using GOGGS as a template for future PFI projects. The consolidation and enhancement of this government workplace have contributed to a reduction in staff turnover and sick days and to an increase in productivity.

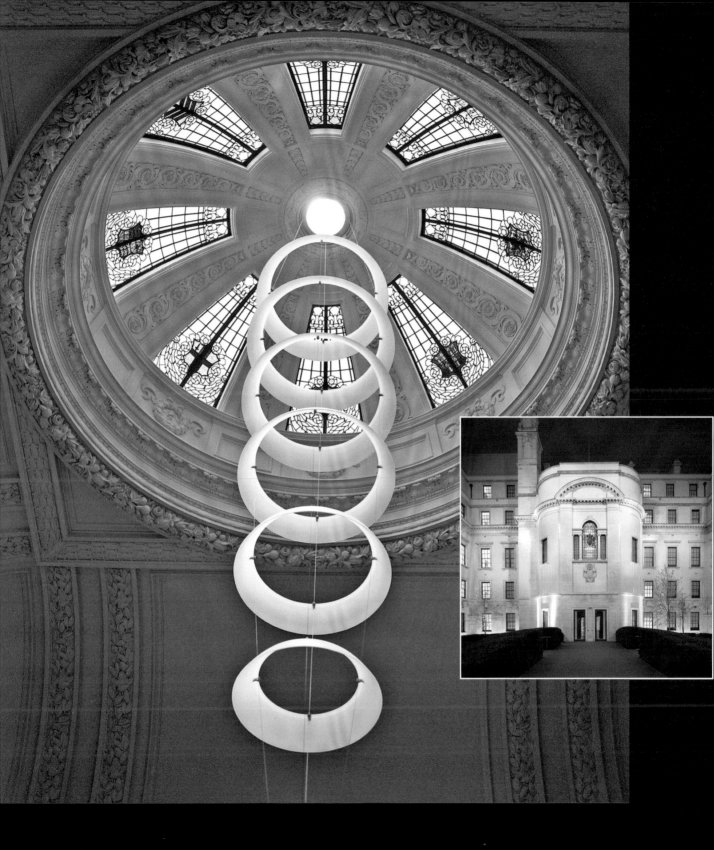

DE HOFTOREN

The Hague, The Netherlands

Development Team

Owner

RGD (Government Building Department)
The Hague, The Netherlands
www.vrom.nl/rijksgebouwendienst

Developer

ING Real Estate Development
The Hague, The Netherlands
www.ingrealestate.com

Architects

Kohn Pedersen Fox Associates (International), PA
London, United Kingdom
www.kpf.com

Arcadis Bouwinfra
The Hague, The Netherlands
www.arcadis.nl

When ING, a real estate development firm based in the Hague, purchased a 0.64-hectare (1.6 ac) parcel in the government/embassy district at the western end of the Malieveld, the city's five-hectare (12 ac) central park, it intended to build an office tower for a large corporate tenant. The prospective development was still a speculative project when the London office of Kohn Pedersen Fox (KPF) won an international design competition conducted by ING. Meanwhile, the Dutch Ministerie van Onderwijs, Cultuur, en Wetenschap (OCW—Ministry of Education, Culture, and Science) was planning to move from a suburban location to the Hague, the country's administrative capital, and it was looking for a suitable headquarters building. Thus ING found a tenant and the development of De Hoftoren became a turnkey operation.

Working with the Rijksgebouwendienst (RGD), the government real estate ownership and management agency representing OCW, and guided by the Urban Regeneration master plan that governs development in this part of the Hague, KPF took the team's design through a number of iterations based on OCW's and RDG's specifications. The final scheme features a single, 29-story tower 144 meters (472 ft) high, the second tallest *wolkenkrabber* (cloud scratcher, a.k.a. skyscraper) in the Netherlands. At street level, a central garden courtyard is embraced on three sides by a 15-story podium and tower—hence the building's name "courtyard tower." The courtyard level opens to a central garden and features a café and an art galleria. A cafeteria on the mezzanine level overlooks the courtyard.

A combination of innovative design responses and mechanical systems optimize De Hoftoren's performance and help satisfy OCW's brief for open, connected, and flexible space. The openness is provided by the building's orientation to the Malieveld, the city center, and the courtyard—aided by the use of transparencies in glass and the design of relationships among discrete spaces. The connectedness is physical as well as visual. A pedestrian bridge built over a canal to expedite the staging of construction work and to link the site with the adjacent rail concourse during construction now eases the passage of people through the property. And the flexibility is built into the workspace design through minimal partitions, large floor plates on the lower levels, and column-free floor plates on the upper levels. These design elements created a satisfied customer. Maria van der Hoeven, minister of OCW, says that De Hoftoren represents "a true reflection of the open and transparent way of working, which is of paramount importance to the ministry." Before the building was complete, RGD negotiated with ING to purchase the building, in which it has installed smaller government agencies as well as OCW.

Although the Dutch landscape is basically horizontal, high densities in urban areas are moving the country in the direction of taller buildings. The Hague already has a few notable *wolkenkrabbers*: the 109-meter (358 ft) Prinsenhof, the 104-meter (341 ft) Castalia refurbished by Michael Graves; and the 88-

meter (289 ft) Zurichtoren designed by Cesar Pelli. The Castalia, built in 1998, was the city's first building taller than 100 meters (328 ft). It disrupted the horizontal Hague skyline with its vertical thrust, but each subsequent *wolkenkrabber* has added legitimacy to the upward-growing skyline and the city's aspirations as a capital.

Not only OCW, but also the public is enthusiastic about the new building, which is seen as a positive new landmark for the city. De Hoftoren is stimulating further redevelopment around it and the adjacent central train station. And RGD is directing two new skyscraper projects that are in development farther to the east.

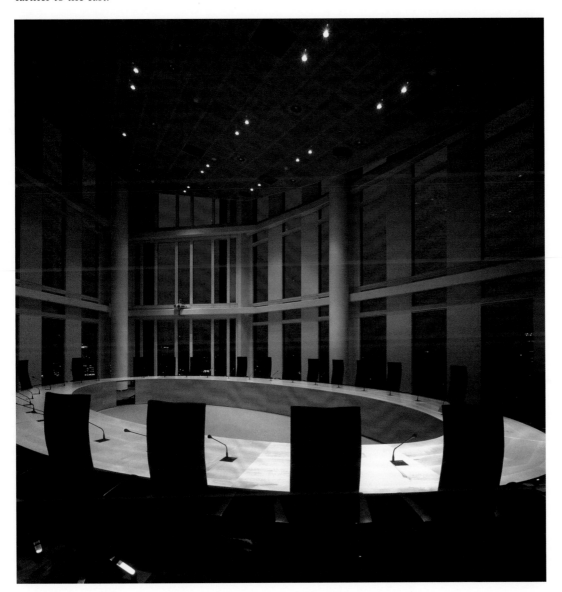

Project Data

Site Area

0.64 hectares (1.6 ac)

Facilities

55,000 square meters (592,000 sf) gross above-grade building area

47,000 square meters (506,000 sf) net building area

370 parking spaces

Land Uses

office, cafeteria, public plaza

Completion Date

November 2002

Jury Statement

Intended to become a leased headquarters building for occupancy by a large corporation, the office tower was purchased from the developer by the Dutch government before its construction was completed. The tower and its podium embrace an inner courtyard (hence the name "Hoftoren" meaning "courtyard tower") that opens to the historic Malieveld park and extends public use to this corner of the Hague's urban parkland.

NIHONBASHI 1-CHOME BUILDING

Tokyo, Japan

Development Team

Owner/Developer

Mitsui Fudosan Company, Ltd.
Tokyo, Japan
www.mitsuifudosan.co.jp

Architects

Kohn Pedersen Fox Associates, PC
New York, New York
www.kpf.com

Nihon Sekkei, Inc.
Tokyo, Japan
www.nihonsekkei.co.jp

Tokyo's Nihonbashi district's importance as the historic center of domestic commerce is embodied in its name, which means "Japan Bridge." Nihonbashi—the bridge—is the zero marker for the national highway system. Economic recession in the 1990s visibly struck the retail establishments in Nihonbashi. Thus, the shuttering in 1999 of the venerable Tokyu department store, which had occupied its site since 1958, was an expected, but unnerving shock. Anxious to keep its other properties in the area from further declining in value, Tokyu—the store's parent company and Japan's second largest railway operator—underwent a corporate restructuring that led to its sale of the defunct department store property to a government-chartered redevelopment agency, Minkan Toshi Kaihatsu Suishin Kiko (which translates as "citizens urban and waterfront development corporation," and contracted to Minkan Toshikiko). Spurred by Minkan Toshikiko's fast-track revitalization schedule, Mitsui Fudosan purchased a half interest in the site and two Tokyu divisions bought back the other half. (Mitsui Fudosan—Japan's largest real estate development firm—is an affiliate of the Mitsui Group conglomerate, which is the largest landowner in the Nihonbashi district.)

Mitsui Fudosan understood the potential of the site, which is prominently located on 1-Chome ("First Street"), atop the Nihonbashi subway station—which was originally built by Tokyu—and between two ancient roads that have morphed into modern-day commercial corridors. With the help of Minkan Toshikiko, the permits for the demolition of the store and the construction of a mixed-use complex were obtained in only three months.

The 121-meter-tall (397 ft) project consists of a five-story podium housing 6,970 square meters (75,024 sf) of leasable retail space for 33 tenants; and a 20-story tower containing 48,725 square meters (524,472 sf) of office space. The low-rise retail block is split by a four-meter-wide (13 ft) pedestrianway that brings shoppers into midblock, which is marked by a 1,500-square-meter (16,146 sf) green space. In order to attract an international investment firm as a flagship tenant, the program included three 4,500-square-meter (48,437 sf) floors of uninterrupted trading space—which is difficult to obtain in central Tokyo. Merrill Lynch has leased this space for its Japan headquarters.

Nihonbashi 1-Chome has remained at 100 percent occupancy since it opened in 2004. After the high-traffic opening days, daily visits have stabilized at 30,000 to 40,000, and traffic at the Nihonbashi subway stop has increased 20 percent. In the one month following the opening, retail sales totaled ¥1 billion ($9.1

Project Data

Site Area **0.82 hectare (2 ac)**

Facilities

**98,064 square meters (1.06 million sf)
total gross area**

**62,225 square meters (669,784 sf)
leasable office space**

**18,727 square meters (201,576 sf)
leasable retail space**

**6,290 square meters (67,705 sf)
graduate school campus**

250 parking spaces

Land Uses **office, retail, institutional, parking**

Completion Date **March 2004**

million), 25 percent more than had been projected. Waseda University's Graduate School of Finance, Accounting, and Law has located its 6,290-square-meter (67,705 sf) campus there.

The development of Nihonbashi 1-Chome took advantage of an opportunity to replace a failed department store building atop a major subway terminal with an architecturally striking office tower and retail block. For the city of Tokyo, the development resolves the intersection at this location of subway lines, commuter-rail lines, and historic streets. For Nihonbashi 1-Chome's anchor tenant, the project provides about 13,500 square meters (145,000 sf) of specialized space that is otherwise unavailable in Tokyo's CBD. And for workers, tourists, and shoppers in downtown, it provides a modern retail amenity that has roots in Nihonbashi's long history as a premier commercial center.

MIXED USE

15/25 DAVIES STREET

London, United Kingdom

Development Team

Owner/Developer

Capital and City, PLC
London, United Kingdom

Architect

Kohn Pedersen Fox Associates
(International), PA
London, United Kingdom
www.kpf.co.uk

Project Data

Web Site

www.the21stmayfair.com

Site Area **743 square meters**
(8,000 sf)

Facilities

5,708 square meters (61,440 sf)
total area

1,152 square meters (12,400 sf)
leasable office space

650 square meters (7,000 sf)
leasable retail space

14 for-sale residential units

16 parking spaces

Land Uses **retail, restaurant,**
office, residential

Completion Date **August 2004**

It is not often that a new project gets built in Mayfair, one of central London's most desirable residential neighborhoods. Much of the land here is owned by the Grosvenor Estate and is occupied under lease-holds that do not encourage the kind of tear-down projects that rejuvenate other cities. And even when a property becomes available, the Westminster planning authority has complete domain over what can be built. The planning authority would be expected to be particularly anxious about any development along Davies Street, which forms a southern gateway to Mayfair from Berkeley Square.

Given this restrictive environment, the design of 15/25 Davies Street is a surprise. But perhaps not that surprising because, despite its obvious parentage in modern architecture, the building blends in sensitively with its historic setting. In form, 15/25 Davies Street fits the archetype of a turn-of-the-century British mansion, but it houses an up-to-date mix of uses that includes a restaurant and shops at street level topped by two office floors and five residential stories. The building's materials are traditional as well, but they are used in decidedly modern ways.

The site is on a busy thoroughfare on the eastern fringe of Mayfair Village. Residents considered the previous 1960s structure to be a misfit in the neighborhood. When the landowner offered the developer, Capital and City, a 50 percent interest in a joint venture for the redevelopment of the site, it was expected that the planning authority would insist on a historical—Victorian or Edwardian—building design. But the careful consideration that the developer gave to the architectural details of a proposed contemporary design—including the use of terra-cotta inside and out, filigreed glass and steel bays on the exterior, and steel stair balustrades on the interior—swayed the authority.

The office entrance faces Davies Street. It is distinct from the individual store entries and from the private entry to the residences. The two levels of office space are directly above the street-level retail/restaurant space. The residential component comprises three two- or three-bedroom units on each of the four stories above the office stories and two units on the penthouse level. They feature multiple balconies and the penthouse units have spacious garden terraces. The 16 parking spaces in the basement are reserved for residents. The residences have sold out, at a high average sale price of £14,693 per square meter ($2,500/£1,365 per sf). The restaurant, the London branch of Venice's Cipriani, and retail spaces were preleased and the office space was leased up within three months of the project's completion.

731 LEXINGTON AVENUE/ ONE BEACON COURT

New York, New York

The completion of this project was the crowning event in the transition of Alexander's from a failed discount retailer to a profitable REIT. In the late 1970s, Interstate Properties, a regional REIT managed by Steven Roth, who is also chairman and CEO of Vornado Realty Trust, started buying up shares in the publicly traded Alexander's, with the declared intention of unlocking the value in the retailer's properties. By the time Alexander's went bankrupt in 1992, Interstate and Vornado together owned more than 60 percent of its common stock. In 1993, Alexander's emerged from bankruptcy repurposed to focus on its biggest asset: the land under its 11 stores. Of most interest was the entire block it owned just south of Bloomingdale's flagship store on Lexington Avenue.

Vornado churned through a succession of development plans, architectural plans, and architects before finally proceeding, six years later, with a mixed-use development plan prepared by Cesar Pelli & Associates that called for a residential, hotel, office, and retail tower. At the time, Bloomberg, LP, the financial news publisher, expressed interest in leasing 450,000 square feet (41,806 m²) of headquarters space, which would make it the anchor tenant. As a lease was about to be signed in late 2000—and after excavation had begun and a foundation had been poured in an effort to beat an impending zoning change that would have imposed a lower height limitation—Bloomberg raised its requirement to 700,000 square feet (65,032 m²). This necessitated a complete redesign of the project, including the elimination of the hotel component and the reorienting of the office component to the more commercial Lexington Avenue.

September 11, 2001, threw a new question into the arena: Would the market for luxury condominiums starting at 475 feet (145 m) in the air be weakened? The development team decided to proceed with the program as planned, which proved to be the correct decision. Manhattan's residential real estate market started on one of its largest upswings ever just as the 105 condominium units of One Beacon Court (the residential component) came on line. Their pricing and absorption exceeded expectations. The average sale price exceeded $2,000 per square foot ($21,529 per m²), and some units—those with views of Central Park—sold in excess of $3,000 per square foot ($32,293 per m²).

Retail leasing has also exceeded the pro forma, and 731 Lexington Avenue (the retail component) has reached 98 percent occupancy. Big-box retailing—which, the developer recognized, lacks suitable space in Manhattan—can be accommodated in two 18-foot-high (5.5 m) subterranean levels, each totaling 75,000 square feet (6,968 m²). Home Depot leases one level (reportedly for $80 per square foot

Development Team

Owner

Alexander's, Inc.
Paramus, New Jersey
www.alx-inc.com

Developer

Vornado Realty Trust
New York, New York
www.vno.com

Architects

Cesar Pelli & Associates
New Haven, Connecticut
www.cesar-pelli.com

SLCE Architects
New York, New York

Project Data

Web Site

www.onebeaconcourt.com

Site Area

1.94 acres (0.78 ha)

Facilities

1.4 million square feet (130,000 m²) total area

885,000 square feet (82,219 m²) leasable office space

174,000 square feet (16,165 m²) leasable retail space

248,000 square feet (20,040 m²) residential condominiums; 105 units

Land Uses

office, retail, residential

Completion Date

mid-2005

Jury Statement

On the site of the former flagship Alexander's department store, this 1.4 million-square-foot (130,000 m²) development—occupying an entire block—now contains offices, luxury condominiums, retail spaces, and Manhattan's first below-grade big-box store. The project's instant success was a deserved reward for the owner's patience and foresight in waiting more than a decade to attract the right developer with the right concept and the right tenants.

($861 per m²) and Bloomberg leases the other for conference, training, and data-center space. Since floor/area ratios in Manhattan are calculated only on above-grade space, the below-grade spaces at 731 Lexington Avenue create enormous value for "free."

Vornado benefited from a zoning bonus under New York City's inclusionary housing program by developing 41 affordable housing units (amounting to 41,000 square feet/3,809 m²) off site. This increased One Beacon Court's FAR from 10 to 12, netting the developer an additional 169,000 square feet (15,701 m²). And the developer received a partial real estate tax exemption under the city's 421(a) program for providing multifamily housing units and supporting off-site affordable housing.

The story of 731 Lexington Avenue/One Beacon Court's development is one of perseverance—the developer's dogged quest to unlock the full value of undervalued real estate and its determination to ride out the vagaries of high-stakes development in New York. Exhibiting the highest level of entrepreneurship throughout the two-decades-long process, Vornado resurrected Alexander's as a hugely profitable company, even without its namesake department stores.

BELMAR

Lakewood, Colorado

Development Team

Owner/Developer

Continuum Partners, LLC
Denver, Colorado
www.continuumpartners.com

Developers

McStain Neighborhoods
Louisville, Colorado
www.mcstain.com

Trammell Crow Residential
Denver, Colorado
www.tcresidential.com

Public Partners

City of Lakewood
Lakewood, Colorado
www.lakewood.org

Lakewood Reinvestment Authority

Mayor's Villa Advisory Committee

Architects

Elkus Manfredi, Ltd.
Boston, Massachusetts
www.elkus-manfredi.com

Van Meter Williams Pollack
Denver, Colorado
www.vmwp.com

Architecture Denver
Denver, Colorado
www.architecturedenver.com

Belmar, a 22-block downtown in the making, exemplifies the potential for transforming post–World War II bedroom suburbs into more diverse, compact, sustainable, pedestrian-oriented, and transit-oriented communities. When completed, it promises to be a model for the redefinition of suburban communities that have been buffeted by inexorable growth over the past several decades.

Lakewood, ten minutes west of Denver, is such a community. With 150,000 people, it is Colorado's fourth largest city. In the early 1900s, wealthy Denver families built country estates there, the largest of which was Belmar. During and after World War II, growth spread west of Denver. In Lakewood, this was spurred by the opening of a federal munitions plant and the Denver Federal Center, which with 10,000 employees in 30 agencies is the largest federal compound outside the Washington, D.C., metropolitan area. In 1966, the 1.4 million-square-foot (130,000 m²) Villa Italia—the largest shopping mall in the mountain/plains region—opened to great fanfare and it became, until its closing in 2001, Lakewood's de facto commercial and civic center.

Long before its actual demise, Villa Italia was clearly dying despite its high-traffic location (80,000 cars passing by its northwest corner each day). But efforts to redevelop it had foundered at the ballot box and been discouraged by a complicated ownership structure involving separate landowners, ground leases, and 140 lease subinterests. However, the process of trying to redevelop the mall had been a learning experience for city officials, who proceeded to form a 30-member Mayor's Villa Advisory Committee (to coordinate development activity) and establish the Lakewood Reinvestment Authority (to provide public financing and other urban renewal resources). Denver-based Continuum Partners was selected by the city as its development partner and worked with these public entities to obtain rezoning, permits, infrastructure financing, and condemnation of the underlying ground lease.

The redevelopment program aims to create for Lakewood a new, 22-block downtown—called Belmar. At buildout, which is projected for 2010 to 2012, the 104-acre (42 ha) site will contain 1.1 million square feet (102,193 m²) of retail, restaurant, and entertainment space; 800,000 square feet (74,322 m²) of office and hotel space; and 1,300 residential units in an urban mix of townhouses, lofts, live/work units, and condominium and rental apartments.

Phase 1 opened in May 2004. It contains 500,000 square feet (46,452 m²) of retail/restaurant/entertainment space with rents that are comparable to regional mall rents—from the high $20s to high $30s per square foot ($300 to $420 per m²), with common area management (CAM) charges in the range of $10 to $15 per square foot ($110 to $160 per m²). Its 184,000 square feet (17,094 m²) of office space is 90 percent occupied in a soft regional office market.

QPK Design
Syracuse, New York
www.qpkdesign.com

Shears Adkins Architects, LLC
Denver, Colorado
www.shearsadkins.com

Belzberg Architects
Santa Monica, California
www.belzbergarchitects.com

Landscape Architects

Civitas, Inc.
Denver, Colorado
www.civitasinc.com

EDAW, Inc.
Denver, Colorado
www.edaw.com

Project Data

Web Site

www.belmarcolorado.com

Site Area

104 acres (42 ha)

Facilities

800,000 square feet (74,322 m²)
leasable office space and hotel

1.1 million square feet (102,193 m²)
leasable retail space

1,300 residential units at buildout

Land Uses

mixed-use retail/restaurant/entertain-
ment, office, hotel, residential

Completion Dates

May 2004 for Phase 1
2010–2012 buildout

Belmar's 109 Phase 1 rental units are 90 percent leased at effective rents of $1.15 to $1.30 per square foot ($12.38 to $14.00 per m²), representing a $.20 to $.30 per square foot ($2.15 to $3.23 per m²) premium over comparable units in the submarket and equivalent to rents being achieved in some of central Denver's best locations. Phase 1's condominium units sold at $245 to $310 per square foot ($2,637 to $3,337 per m²) and the first 70 rowhouses sold for an average price of more than $360,000. These Phase 1 results are unprecedented in the local market.

This snapshot of leasing and sales activity demonstrates that interest is high and that people are beginning to take ownership of the Belmar concept. Phase 2, which is currently under construction, will add 250,000 square feet (23,226 m²) of retail/restaurant/entertainment space and 500 housing units.

All buildings in Belmar feature ground-level windows and doors on all sides to enhance the streetscape and the pedestrian experience. A segment of one street can be closed off temporarily to accommodate a public market. A 15,000-square-foot (1,394 m²) contemporary-arts center is under construction. A multi-tenant, speculative office building has earned a silver certification from the U.S. Green Building Council's Leadership in Energy and Environmental Design (LEED) building rating program. Such features and design choices indicate that Belmar celebrates the public realm over the private realm. At Belmar, streets are more important than any buildings on them and parks and plazas are more important than the buildings that surround them.

THE BRIDGE 8

Shanghai, People's Republic of China

Development Team

Owner/Developer

**Life Style Centre Limited
Shanghai, People's Republic of China**

Architect

**HMA Architects & Designers, Ltd.
Shanghai, People's Republic of China
www.hma.if.tv**

Project Data

Web Site **www.bridge8.com**

Site Area **0.7 hectare (1.73 ac)**

Facilities

**12,000 square meters (129,167 sf)
gross building area**

**8,335 square meters (89,717 sf)
total leasable area**

**1,887 square meters (20,311 sf)
leasable office space**

**6,448 square meters (69,406 sf)
leasable retail/restaurant space**

**830 square meters (8,934 sf) exterior
open space**

Land Uses

office, restaurants, retail

Completion Date **December 2004**

To Tony Wong, president of Life Style Centre Limited, a cluster of abandoned factory buildings in the bustling Luwan district in downtown Shanghai represented an opportunity to fill a need. They could be redeveloped as office/studio space for creative professionals—designers, advertisers, and marketers. "Though China is emerging as the world's manufacturing powerhouse, it is not yet known for originality and creativity, which are cornerstones for the sustainable development of an economy," said Wong. "Around the world, cities that are known for creativity attract creative people. They flock together to trigger mutual inspiration."

With 22 office/studio tenants including Skidmore, Owings & Merrill (U.S. architects), F-emotion (French public relations agency), Aedas (Beijing architects), ALSOP (British architects), and INFIX (Japanese design consultants), The Bridge 8 has succeeded in bringing creative, cosmopolitan tenants to Shanghai.

The 50-year-old buildings, which had been used as workshops by a car manufacturer, were in disrepair. Their blight represented an urban planning headache for the district, while their prime location would require a buyer to make a heavy investment. Instead, Wong obtained a 20-year lease on the site, at the end of which the real estate would revert to the owner. His plan was to retain the shells, adding and subtracting external and internal elements that would tie the structures together. This redevelopment scheme meshed with the district government's plan to retain the historical character of the neighborhood, and the government's cooperation in securing approvals and generally assisting the project kept the construction period to less than nine months.

The word "bridge" in the project's name alludes to a number of project elements, including its exterior skybridges and walkways, the corridors and catwalks that connect the interiors of the buildings, the bridge between past and present that adaptive use represents, and the global industry that this project— and Shanghai in general—hoped to attract.

The industrial origins of the buildings are visible in the refurbishment. Steel trusses and load-bearing walls are exposed. The design interventions are modern and include skylights, glass curtain walls and storefronts, cantilevered staircases, stainless-steel rails and balustrades, mezzanines, balconies, and bays. Common facilities for meetings and promotions open the interior spaces even more, exterior spaces between buildings provide informal meeting places, and retail space—comprising five restaurants and nine stores—is scattered throughout the complex.

Total development costs were RMB 25 million ($3 million). The payback period for the 20-year lease is projected to be five years, for a final internal rate of return (IRR) of more than 30 percent. Now fully leased, The Bridge 8 was 90 percent leased before it was completed.

LA CITTADELLA

Kawasaki, Japan

Development Team

Owner/Developer

Citta Entertainment Co., Ltd.
Kawasaki, Japan

Architects

The Jerde Partnership
Venice, California
www.jerde.com

Ishimoto Architects
Tokyo, Japan
www.ishimoto.co.jp

Landscape Architects

EDAW, Inc.
San Francisco, California
www.edaw.com

Project Data

Web Site **www.lacittadella.co.jp**

Site Area **1.6 hectares (4 ac)**

Facilities

23,690 square meters (255,000 sf) gross leasable area

500 parking spaces

Land Uses **restaurants, retail, nightclub, cineplex**

Completion Date **November 2002**

La Cittadella ("citadel" in Italian) is more than a clever use of an Italian theme for an entertainment and retail complex centered on a historic nightclub, Club Citta, and Japan's first multiplex, Cinecitta. With its abstracted replication of a hillside town in Italy, the project brings to mind the kind of street life that animates such towns. Although superficially it may be reminiscent of a movie set, it is actually a serious expression of Japan's cultural affinity for all things western, as well as an innovative infill project that not only reinforces Kawasaki city's urban design plan, but also offers residents an alternative town center.

Kawasaki is a historically industrial city located at the midpoint of the Tokyo/Yokohama conurbation. In order to enhance the economic return on its investment, Citta Entertainment, operator of the historic Club Citta and Cinecitta—social landmarks for the young and trendy in Kawasaki—decided to temporarily close down in order to redevelop the site at a higher density. The owner turned to the Jerde Partnership, a California-based architecture firm that was establishing itself in Asia as a designer of innovative "experiential" retail environments. Jerde's plan was for a vertical entertainment center that could achieve the highest allowable floor/area ratio (FAR) that would continue the Italian branding for the circulation and design motifs.

At La Cittadella customers are drawn upward past the retail tenants, until they find themselves at the top—10.5 meters (34 ft) above the street—from where they can enjoy a panoramic view of the otherwise flat coastal city and all of La Cittadella. A 4.5-meter-wide (15 ft) outdoor path that slopes at a reasonable 4 percent grade and extends 260 meters (853 ft) in a meandering, switchback fashion facilitates the climbing experience. Animated with foot traffic, the path appears and disappears from view, summoning one's curiosity. Along the way, landscaped terraces, bridges, stepped gardens, and outdoor seating evoke an Italian village alive with nighttime activity. These streetscaping elements and the retail stores back up to the windowless facades of the cineplex, helping to articulate what otherwise would have been blank walls.

Citta Entertainment's strategy for increasing the value of the site is supported by a high ratio of restaurants in the retail mix—17 in all, occupying 2,980 square meters (32,076 sf) scattered along the outdoor path and offering alfresco dining. Between the restaurants is tucked 2,044 square meters (22,000 sf) of retail space. At the base of the complex sits a 2,500-square-meter (26,910 sf) semicircular amphitheater surrounding a fountain that is used for animated water and light shows. After a two-year absence during construction, the 2,833-square-meter (30,494 sf) club and the 13-screen cinema have returned.

Since opening in November 2002, La Cittadella has drawn more than 4 million visitors a year—and the relocated Cinecitta has continued to be Japan's busiest Cineplex with 1.95 million patrons in its first year. All the center's restaurants and retail spaces are fully leased and occupied.

FOURTH STREET LIVE!

Louisville, Kentucky

The nighttime and weekend entertainment concentrated at Fourth Street Live! has reenergized Louisville's downtown and helped jump-start a residential and tourism resurgence. The project turned a city-owned liability into a tax- and job-generating asset. How it came to be developed is an instructive story that involves the convergence of political will, developer savvy, and stakeholder cooperation around a civic need.

Riding the wave of urban regeneration in the late 1990s, downtown Louisville was making progress, but it was missing one critical element—an entertainment district. Downtown had scattered entertainment venues, a solid supply of hotel rooms, restaurants, a popular convention center, and even an about-to-be waterfront park along its Ohio River frontage. And it had a not-so-old enclosed mall, the Louisville Galleria, that looked vacant—even if it was eking out a survival—and stood as a physical and psychological symbol of downtown's hard times.

The Galleria was built in 1982 in an effort to attract customers away from suburban malls and back to downtown. Straddling Fourth Street, the mall featured a glass atrium of open-web steel joists that spanned the width of the street and closed off a block of one of downtown's main streets.

But the novelty of a downtown shopping center wore off and the mall dwindled to irrelevance. By late 2000, it was evident that the mall's owners would not invest in its redevelopment. After issuing a request for proposals (RFP) for its redevelopment, the city awarded development rights to the Cordish Company. The developer negotiated a complex public/private partnership with the city along the lines of the partnership agreements under which Cordish had developed comparable projects in Houston (Bayou Place), Baltimore (Power Plant), and Atlantic City (The Walk).

The transformation of the Galleria into Fourth Street Live! hinged on reopening Fourth Street to vehicular traffic (but installing disappearing barriers so that the block could be closed at night, on weekends, and for festivals); retaining the glass atrium roof over the street; and converting the vacant six-story Kaufman Straus department store building, a historic building that was located in the heart of the project, to office space. The Kaufman Straus renovation added 80,000 square feet (7,432 m²) of office space to the 270,000 square feet (25,084 m²) of retail space captured in the reconfiguration of the Galleria.

The total development cost for Fourth Street Live! was approximately $72 million. The city contributed $13 million in bonds, of which $4 million was used to buy the Galleria. The state agreed to rebate new sales taxes generated by the project up to $700,000 a year for ten years. It also granted Fourth Street Live! an arena liquor license so that patrons can walk around with alcoholic beverages.

The developer has met regional and local market expectations with a mix of national chains and a high proportion (25 percent) of local tenants. Extensive soft programming—170 free live events sched-

Development Team

Owner/Developer

The Cordish Company
Baltimore, Maryland
www.cordish.com

Architects

Beyer Blinder Belle
New York, New York
www.beyerblinderbelle.com

Bravura Architecture
Louisville, Kentucky

uled in the project's first year—give it a Louisvillian flavor. Cordish relies as well on property management and investment to ensure that the entertainment offerings remain fresh and interesting.

Fourth Street Live! attracted more than 4.2 million visitors in its first year, making it the most visited destination in Kentucky. The development is 98 percent leased, and retail tenants were paying percentage rent in their first year. The project is generating $3 million annually in new tax revenue, it has helped catalyze more than $200 million in private investment throughout the downtown area, and it has directly created 1,500 new jobs.

Project Data

Web Site

www.4thstlive.com

Site Area

8 acres (3.2 ha)

Facilities

400,000 square feet (37,161 m²)
total area

270,000 square feet (25,084 m²)
gross leasable retail space

80,000 square feet (7,432 m²)
gross leasable office space

1,200 parking spaces

Land Uses

retail, entertainment, office, parking

Completion Date

September 2004

Jury Statement

The developer revitalized a failed enclosed mall downtown, and in the process catalyzed further redevelopment in Louisville. Packed with entertainment programming, Fourth Street Live! is an entertainment and retail center that has become a magnet for nighttime downtown activity.

HANGZHOU WATERFRONT

Hangzhou, People's Republic of China

Those familiar with the Embarcadero district in San Francisco will immediately understand the significance of the Hangzhou waterfront development. Like the Embarcadero, Hangzhou's Hubin district—the city's major waterfront district on the eastern shore of West Lake—was cut off from the lakefront by a freeway. Unlike the Embarcadero Freeway, however, Hangzhou's waterfront highway was on grade, and the lakefront had seen no development. To capture the lakefront for urban use, then, was not merely a matter of removing the highway, but also of planning for development that could maximize the lakefront's potential as a recreational and commercial amenity.

Hangzhou, an important tourist destination in China, is 180 kilometers (112 mi) southwest of Shanghai. It has served ancient emperors as a capital city and is still a cultural center. To the Chinese, Hangzhou's West Lake is as familiar an icon as the Great Wall or the Forbidden City. Marco Polo visited Hangzhou in the late 13th century and called the city "beyond dispute the finest and the noblest in the world." For the Chinese, a pilgrimage to Hangzhou is an essential life experience. Of the 30 million tourists who visit West Lake each year, 2 million are foreigners.

Hubin Road, a multilane freeway that grew out of scale as Hangzhou began participating in China's "economic miracle," left only a narrow strip of lakefront land available for public use and benefited only the owners of property facing the water. The Hangzhou government formed a public/private partnership, the Hangzhou Hubin Commerce & Tourism Company, tasked with making the waterfront more of a

Development Team

Owner/Developer

Hangzhou Hubin Commerce & Tourism Company, Ltd.
Hangzhou, People's Republic of China
www.eurostreet.com.cn

Planner

SWA Group
Houston, Texas
www.swagroup.com

Architects

Zhejiang South Architecture Design Company
Hangzhou, People's Republic of China

Jerde Partnership
Venice, California
www.jerde.com

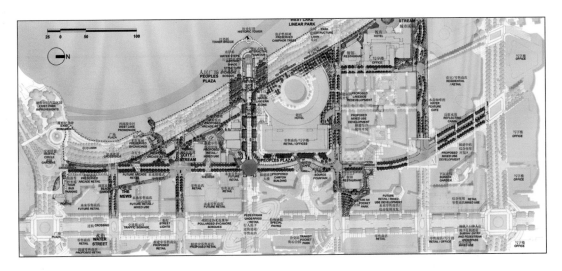

Project Data

Web Site

www.eurostreet.com.cn

Site Area

12.7 hectares (31 ac)

Facilities

21,272 square meters (228,977 sf)
land occupied by buildings

41,343 square meters (445,027 sf)
retail space

12,607 square meters (135,705 sf)
office space

Land Uses

waterfront park, retail, office, hotel

Completion Date

October 2003

Jury Statement

The city of Hangzhou has put West Lake—storied in Chinese poetry and legend—on the international map through a large-scale public improvement of its scenic waterfront. The lively mixed-use development and pedestrian-oriented spaces have given Hangzhou's citizens a new amenity that is environmentally sensitive and encourages new high-quality development.

tourist amenity. The SWA Group of Houston and Zhejiang South Architecture Design Company, a local firm, were invited to produce a master plan. The government was to bear 60 percent of the development costs, with private entities contributing the balance.

The first obstacle to be corrected was Hubin Road. Through-traffic was redirected to a four-lane, 1.5-kilometer-long (0.9 mi) tunnel under the lakebed approximately 40 meters (130 ft) from the shoreline, which opened the road for use as a multipurpose, pedestrian-friendly boulevard. A 650-meter-long by 40-meter-wide (2,132×131 ft) tree-lined park was designed to mediate between the shoreline and the new boulevard. "City streams" weaving through the district were constructed, recalling the natural streams that once coursed through Hubin and directing pedestrians toward the lake.

Development in the Hubin district totaling 53,950 square meters (580,732 sf) of commercial space has occurred in response to Hangzhou's waterfront improvements. A lakeside international hotel and entertainment venues are located at the boulevard's center. Not counting the lakeside linear park, public open space within the developed blocks east of Hubin Road occupies 27 percent of the land area.

The Hangzhou waterfront project is an outstanding example of a public/private partnership formed to advance a public good and provide opportunities for private real estate development. Its success has been noted by cities across the nation and is being studied for emulation.

THE JEFFERSON
AT PENN QUARTER

Washington, D.C.

The Jefferson at Penn Quarter in downtown Washington, D.C., made use of historic facades to create a mixed-use block that respects the history of its site while providing significant urban amenities. Its development encountered many challenges, but it is expected that the rewards for the developer will be commensurate with the high risks.

Owned by the U.S. General Services Administration (GSA), the project site was one of the last remaining eyesores in the East End/Penn Quarter neighborhood, which has undergone significant reinvestment since the days when the Pennsylvania Avenue Development Corporation was in place. The MCI Center, a professional sports arena and entertainment complex, is two blocks to the north. The National Portrait Gallery, the FBI building, two major retail/office/residential developments—Market Square and the Lansburgh—and two Metrorail subway stops are also within a two-block radius.

JPI's plan won out over 19 other responses to GSA's request for proposals (RFP). The site, almost a full block, included 13 historic properties along three street fronts. The RFP had called for the preservation of the historic facades. JPI satisfied this requirement with a preservation option known as "facadectomy"— the preservation of the facades only and the construction of a new structure behind them—which facilitated the approval process in a city known for its protracted design scrutiny of historic properties. The project included the restoration of the original 1885 facade and entrance of one of the buildings on the site; the restoration and reuse of the building that served as Clara Barton's Civil War headquarters; and the restoration of eight additional facades—four of which were suspended in mid-air while their foundations were reconstructed, put back on the upgraded foundations, and then restored in place; and four of which were disassembled, restored off site, and reinstalled. A new ten-story structure was built behind the restored facades and buildings to accommodate housing, ground-floor retail, a 250-seat theater, and a parking garage.

A number of specialty shops—including a national coffee chain, a high-end salon, and a white-tablecloth restaurant—have signed leases and have begun fitting out their spaces behind the preserved facades. The Clara Barton museum located in her restored headquarters will be operated by the GSA. A 250-seat performing-arts theater is the new home of the Woolly Mammoth Theatre Company, an established local theater. In a city in which federal law prohibits the construction of municipal parking garages, the inclusion of a 450-space subterranean parking garage was welcome.

The developer originally intended to rent all 428 units at market rate. But an updated analysis of the market while the project was under construction led JPI to convert two-fifths (173 units) to condominiums. After repackaging these 173 units as The Lafayette and selling 156 of them in just two months at prices exceeding $410 per square foot ($4,413 per m²), JPI converted the remaining 255 units to condominiums, naming them The Clara Barton. Most units were sold out in three months at prices exceeding $425 per square foot ($4,575 per m²). The Lafayette and The Clara Barton have their own entrances, but they share all residential amenities.

A landscaped courtyard surrounded on three sides by the new building serves all the uses. A rooftop pool and terrace are residential amenities. The residential component is marketed to professionals who are attracted by being able to walk to work, having access to two Metro stations, and living in an emerging entertainment district.

Development Team

Owner/Developer

JPI
McLean, Virginia
www.jpi.com

Architect

Esocoff & Associates
Washington, D.C.
www.esocoff.com

Project Data

Site Area **1.74 acres (0.7 ha)**

Facilities

35,000 square feet (3,252 m²)
leasable retail space

428 condominium housing units

250-seat performing-arts theater

450 parking spaces

Land Uses **residential, theater,**
museum, retail/restaurant

Completion Date **summer 2005**

THE MARKET COMMON, CLARENDON

Arlington, Virginia

Among the commercial corridors radiating out from Washington, D.C., the Rosslyn-Ballston corridor is unique in being served along its entire length by a Metrorail line. The post-subway development that has occurred along this spine has sometimes leapfrogged from one commercial center to another, leaving a number of underutilized segments with intact nearby residential enclaves. The Market Common, Clarendon, fills one such void with a mixed-use development providing stores and restaurants, office space, housing, public open space, and public parking.

This portion of Clarendon Boulevard was a thriving shopping and restaurant district before the corridor began evolving into an urban street characterized by higher building densities. By the time The Market Common was being planned, the project area had fallen into decline and much of the land was used for surface parking. However, any redevelopment proposals—including one for a retail center anchored by a big-box store—met with distrust from the residential neighborhoods located on both sides of the commercial strip. Arlington County tried to encourage redevelopment by adopting a master plan, which was approved by the affected neighborhoods. But the plan reflected development goals more than it did market realities.

McCaffery Interests, a Chicago developer with recent experience in the metropolitan Washington area, believed that the goals of the master plan could be accommodated with the right mix of commercial tenants and land uses, and it set about assembling the 18 acres (7.3 ha) as four separate parcels. After six months of meetings—40 with neighborhood and community groups and 50 with government agencies—a plan for a town center emerged. The critical breakthrough was the idea of opening an inward-facing retail center to Clarendon Boulevard and placing outward-facing housing on the three sides that are on residential streets—leaving no blank facades and maximizing the street frontage of the commercial center.

The development's residential periphery blends in with the surroundings in use and in character. A one-acre (0.4 ha) landscaped strip that is dedicated to public use further buffers the development from the neighborhood. Thirty townhouses front this park and walkways connect 57 mews-style townhouses occupying a second side of the block to the commercial area. Thus, the development is permeable to residents of the surrounding neighborhood, who, because they can walk through the residential periphery to get to the commercial center, do not experience the full-block project as an obstruction between the

Development Team

Owner

TIAA-CREF
Charlotte, North Carolina
www.tiaa-cref.org

Developer

McCaffery Interests, Inc.
Chicago, Illinois
www.mccafferyinterests.com

Townhouse Developer

Eakin Youngentob Associates
Arlington, Virginia
www.eya.com

Architect

Antunovich Associates
Chicago, Illinois
www.antunovich.com

Project Data

Web Site **www.marketcc.com**

Site Area **18 acres (7.3 ha)**

Facilities

1,232,181 square feet (114,473 m²) total area

101,337 square feet (9,415 m²) gross leasable office space

303,150 square feet (28,164 m²) gross leasable retail space

387 total residential units: 87 townhouses, 300 rental apartments

1,554 parking spaces

Land Uses

residential, retail/restaurant/entertainment, office, park and open space, parking

Completion Date

November 2003

Jury Statement

The Market Common, Clarendon, is a classic win-win development. Benefiting from the development momentum spurred by growth along a Metrorail subway corridor, this 18-acre (7.3 ha), mixed-use project responds sensitively to its neighborhood's residential context, and contributes a public park and an open space in the center, as well as much-needed structured and street parking—all successfully integrated with 387 for-sale and for-rent residential units.

commercial land uses on Clarendon Boulevard and the residential neighborhoods behind them. The for-sale townhouses have back-alley vehicular access. A ten-story building with 300 for-rent apartment units occupies the third residential side.

The Market Common is primarily experienced, however, as a retail development facing Clarendon Boulevard. A U-shaped drive brings vehicular traffic into the parklike 150-foot-wide (46 m) central area around which is placed 216,000 square feet (20,067 m²) of retail and restaurant space. The upper stories contain 101,337 square feet (9,415 m²) of leasable office space. A parking structure containing 1,368 spaces meets parking demand from The Market Common as well as nearby businesses that otherwise rely on street parking. Parallel parking—36 spaces—on the U-drive access gives a neighborhood feel to the stores along the interior street.

McCaffery has developed an additional 58,000 square feet (5,388 m²) of retail space and 150 structured parking spaces across and along Clarendon Boulevard. The developer estimates that The Market Common has catalyzed nearly $1 billion in new development in its immediate vicinity. The project's financial returns have been impressive: It cost approximately $150 million to develop, was sold to TIAA-CREF at a handsome profit, and is yielding steady returns to its new owner. But it has yielded even more benefits to the Clarendon neighborhood, which has lost an eyesore and gained a town center.

MARUNOUCHI BUILDING

Tokyo, Japan

A symbol of Japan's aspirations as a world power since its completion in 1923, the Marunouchi Building—popularly known as "Marubiru" (a contraction of "Marunouchi Building")—began its reincarnation in 1995 when three events coalesced to make redevelopment an urgency: a major development project was needed to catalyze a public/private redevelopment plan that had been adopted for Tokyo's CBD; structural studies undertaken in the aftermath of a major earthquake in Kobe earlier that year had revealed Marubiru's inadequacies; and Marubiru's owner was positioned to capitalize on the building's popularity and iconic status.

The 120-hectare (297 ac) Marunouchi district encompasses Tokyo's central train station (the embarkation point for the so-called bullet train) and the entrance to the 101-hectare (250 ac) Imperial Palace. (The name "Marunouchi" means "within the [castle] walls.") The approximately 4,100 companies that have offices in Marunouchi are responsible for nearly 20 percent of Japan's gross domestic product.

Ever since 1890, when Mitsubishi rescued the national government from financial crisis by purchasing 36 hectares (89 ac) near the Imperial Palace, the company has remained a major property owner in the district and, at the time of Marubiru's expansion, Mitsubishi owned 31 of the 98 commercial properties there. It therefore had the strongest of incentives to work to upgrade the district, which was a top business address but lagged as a nighttime and weekend destination. Marubiru was a landmark structure not only for its premier location, but also for its size and for its status as Japan's first western-style office building with street-level retail space.

Mitsubishi took advantage of its dominating landlord position in Marunouchi to maximize the development potential of Marubiru by leading a consortium of the district's 89 landowners and city agencies wanting to leverage the economic potential of the district. By contributing public spaces and streetscape improvements, and by transferring development rights from an adjacent building, Mitsubishi was able to increase Marubiru's floor area from 64,000 to 160,000 square meters (688,890 to 1.7 million sf) and its height from 31 to 180 meters (102 to 591 ft). By temporarily or permanently relocating tenants to nearby buildings it owned, Mitsubishi was able to offset some of the loss of rental revenue during reconstruction.

The Marubiru that rose in place of the original Marubiru retains only its footprint. The eight-story podium is pared to five stories, but atop the podium is a new 31-story tower. A new foundation replaces

Development Team

Owner/Developer

Mitsubishi Estate Company, Ltd.
Tokyo, Japan
www.mec.co.jp

Architect

Mitsubishi Jisho Sekkei, Inc.
Tokyo, Japan
www.mj-sekkei.com

Project Data

Web Site www.marubiru.jp

Site Area 1 hectare (2.47 ac)

Facilities

160,000 square meters (1,722,226 sf)
gross building area

76,215 square meters (820,371 sf)
gross leasable area

53,600 square meters (576,946 sf)
leasable office space

21,000 square meters (226,042 sf)
leasable retail space

409 parking spaces

Land Uses office, retail, restaurant,
entertainment, parking

Completion Date August 2002

Jury Statement

As Japan's first modern office building, the Marunouchi Building was a landmark in 1923. Today, with the construction within the original footprint of a 31-story tower atop a five-story podium, the building resumes its landmark status, setting a new high standard for historic preservation, upgrading the character and value of its central Tokyo neighborhood, attracting new nightlife and weekend activity, and providing a model for the revitalization of CBDs everywhere.

5,443 pine piles, all of which were removed and one of which has been preserved for historic display. Also retained were the iconic triple arches that were built into Marubiru's original facade, which symbolized the name "Mitsubishi" (meaning "three water chestnuts"), a symbol that has been stylized as diamond shapes in the company's logo. Marubiru contains four subterranean levels, which provide retail space, pedestrian connections to Tokyo station, and parking for 409 cars under the adjacent streets. Each floor of the new tower is a column-free 2,000 square meters (21,527 sf). Most of the tower is leased as office space.

A year before the project's completion, 100 percent of the office space was preleased at more than twice the average lease rates for office space in Tokyo's five major wards. The office and retail space continues to be fully leased, and the project's success has encouraged five owners of major buildings in Marunouchi to redevelop their properties. The Marubiru project cost ¥58 billion ($525 million), and Mitsubishi plans to invest a total of ¥500 billion ($4 billion) over the next ten years in Marunouchi to redevelop six buildings and continue its streetfront improvement program. Approximately 240,000 people work in the Marunouchi district. Almost all of them pass through Tokyo station every day, and 55,000 use the rebuilt Marubiru's wide range of facilities.

Marubiru's redevelopment sets new standards for urban mixed-use developments and, by enhancing street life, the building is radiating positive economic effects throughout the Marunouchi district. Furthermore, Marubiru's financial success has encouraged the Japanese government to continue its deregulation of the economy and to act creatively in maximizing efficiency in urban land use.

WINNER · MIXED USE

TIME WARNER CENTER

New York, New York

No single building complex since Rockefeller Center has had the opportunity to exert such a positive impact on New York City. In July 1998, the Metropolitan Transportation Authority selected the development team—a partnership of the Related Companies, LP, and Apollo Real Estate Advisors, LP—to redevelop the approximately 3.4-acre (1.38 ha) site of the demolished New York Coliseum on Columbus Circle in the heart of Manhattan. The development team put together a dynamic and synergistic mix of components, generous public spaces, and breathtaking views to capitalize on this exceptional location that is the gateway to midtown Manhattan, the Upper West Side, and Central Park. Time Warner Center is a city within a building more than it is a building within a city.

"I believe Time Warner Center will become the most important mixed-use development in New York City, creating a new cultural center that will deliver an unrivaled experience in which people will dine, shop, live, work, and be entertained in a unique and exciting complex at one of the world's most visible and prominent locations," says Kenneth A. Himmel, president and CEO of Related Urban Development. The uses include office and broadcast facilities occupied by Time Warner, multiple levels of retail space, destination specialty restaurants, condominium residences, a hotel (Mandarin Oriental), three performance halls totaling 1,970 seats and other facilities for Jazz at Lincoln Center, and one-of-a-kind public spaces.

Time Warner Center's form and imagery are derived from the Manhattan street grid. A stone-and-glass podium houses seven stories of retail and studio space—in which the high level of people activity appears to mirror that going on outside on Broadway—topped by broadcasting studios and office space.

Development Team

Owner/Developer

The Related Companies, LP
New York, New York
www.related.com

Owners

Apollo Real Estate Advisors, LP
New York, New York
www.apollorealestate.com

Mandarin Oriental Hotel Group
Hong Kong
www.mandarin-oriental.com

Time Warner, Inc.
New York, New York
www.timewarner.com/corp

Jazz at Lincoln Center
New York, New York
www.jazzatlincolncenter.org

Architects

Skidmore, Owings & Merrill, LLP
New York, New York
www.som.com

Elkus Manfredi Architects, Ltd.
Boston, Massachusetts
www.elkus-manfredi.com

Brennan Beer Gorman Architects
New York, New York
www.bbg-bbgm.com

Ismael Leyva Architects, PC
New York, New York
www.ilarch.com

Rafael Viñoly Architects, PC
New York, New York
www.rvapc.com

Project Data

Web Sites

www.onecentralpark.com

www.shopsatcolumbuscircle.com

Site Area **3.4 acres (1.38 ha)**

Facilities

2.8 million square feet (260,130 m²) total area

1.1 million square feet (102,190 m²) leasable office/studio/broadcast space

340,000 square feet (31,590 m²) leasable retail space

1,970 seats in three performance halls

201 residential condominiums

251 hotel keys

504 parking spaces

Land Uses **residential, hotel, retail, office/studio/broadcast, performance halls, parking**

Completion Date **October 2004**

Jury Statement

Time Warner Center represents a positive resolution to the decades-long controversy over what to do about Columbus Circle, at the southwest corner of Central Park. This 2.8 million-square-foot (260,130 m²), mixed-use project has provided the city with a landmark worthy of its unique location, and with a hugely successful magnet for investment.

Set back on the base, a pair of office and residential towers culminate in luminous glass crowns 750 feet (229 m) above Columbus Circle. The main public entrance, a giant window, opens into a 150-foot-high (46 m) atrium that showcases the retail, restaurant, and entertainment space. The window opens the building to Central Park, so that visitors can experience the same dramatic views of the park that office tenants and residents enjoy. Additional contributions made to the public realm include space donated to Jazz at Lincoln Center, the rebuilding of a subway station, and a contribution to the $20 million landscaping makeover of Columbus Circle.

A creative ownership structure—a condominium regime in which each of seven owners has a fee interest in its condominium unit—helped finance the project. All project components are exceeding financial expectations. The Shops at Columbus Circle is realizing net rents of up to $450 per square foot ($4,844 per m²) and nearly every merchant is exceeding sales expectations. The hotel has already become the city's rate leader. Most of the office/studio/broadcast space is occupied, primarily by Time Warner. And One Central Park—the residential component—is achieving sale prices of almost $2,500 per square foot ($27,000 per m²), with sales expected to exceed projections by 25 percent. In early 2005, all but ten of the 201 condominiums had been sold.

HOUSING

900 PENN AVENUE APARTMENTS

Pittsburgh, Pennsylvania

Development Team

Owner/Developer

TREK Development Group, Inc.
Pittsburgh, Pennsylvania
www.trekdevelopment.com

Architect

Thomas R. Harley Architects, LLC
Indiana, Pennsylvania

Project Data

Web Site **www.900penn.com**

Site Area **6,000 square feet (557 m²)**

Facilities

4,700 square feet (437 m²) retail space

25 rental housing units

Land Uses **residential, retail**

Completion Date **January 1999**

The core of Pittsburgh's cultural district occupies eight blocks (two blocks by four blocks) along the southern, downtown side of the Allegheny River. The world-class orchestra, dance, theater, and opera companies that make a home here were created by Industrial Age capital and have continued to thrive into the present, supported by benefactors like the Carnegie, Mellon, and Heinz Foundations. The neighborhood itself has had its ups and downs—going from theater district to adult entertainment district to revived cultural district—with much of the credit for its latest revival owed to the efforts of the Pittsburgh Cultural Trust, an arts agency and real estate and economic development catalyst established in 1984 by prominent local foundations and other civic leaders to revitalize this area of downtown Pittsburgh.

Bringing people downtown to live was an early goal of the Pittsburgh Cultural Trust, although this was a difficult proposition in the cultural district because historic preservation laws made it difficult to renovate many of its commercial buildings for residential use and rents were not nearly high enough to justify the high cost of such renovations. Federal laws that prohibit the intermingling of charitable trust funds—like those from the nonprofit arts foundations that had the most interest in the district—with for-profit development ventures added a further complication.

In 1997, William J. Gatti, Jr., president of TREK Development Group, Inc., a housing developer and patron of the cultural district, approached the Cultural Trust with a plan to renovate the vacant William G. Johnston building for residential use. Located on a corner, the building is a six-story, timber-frame and masonry structure that had been constructed in 1890 as a printing factory. Intrigued by the proposal, the Cultural Trust optioned the building from the bank that had taken it back on bankruptcy and conducted a competition to solicit additional development schemes.

TREK's plan was to convert the building from its last use as offices to ground-floor retail and 25 residences on floors two through six while restoring the original exterior. The Pittsburgh Public Theatre made a 15-year commitment to rent 12 of the planned residential units for use by the company's guest actors; the city's Urban Redevelopment Authority provided a facade-restoration grant; and the developer obtained tax credits for the historic restoration of the building's exterior—all of which made it possible for TREK to assemble a plausible pro forma for the development. On these strengths, the Cultural Trust awarded the development rights to TREK and took a third position on a $600,000 loan to finance TREK's purchase of the building from the Trust.

The development preserved and refurbished many of the original elements of the building, including its wood-and-tin ceilings and exposed-brick interior walls. A number of elements that had been lost over the years—such as the arched windows and cornices—were reconstructed. Since 900 Penn Avenue opened in 1999, the residential units—which range in size from 870-square-foot (81 m²) studios to 2,300-square-foot (214 m²) two-bedroom apartments—have been at 100 percent occupancy. The 4,700-square-foot (437 m²) commercial space at street level has been occupied since 2004 by a restaurant.

As the first for-rent residential project in downtown Pittsburgh in more than 15 years, 900 Penn Avenue led a resurgence in downtown housing. A number of other development initiatives outside the cultural district over the past decade—among them, a waterfront park adjoining the cultural district, two sports venues across the river and a short walk away via one of several picturesque bridges, and a convention center at the eastern edge of the cultural district—also have helped bring a new vibrancy to downtown.

THE LOFT

Singapore

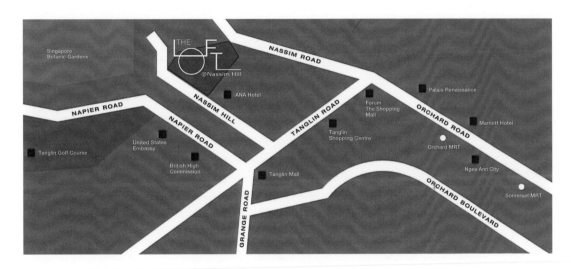

Development Team

Owner/Developer

CapitaLand Residential, Ltd.
Singapore
www.capitaland.com.sg

Architect

W Architects
Singapore

Landscape Architect

Tierra Design (S) Pte, Ltd.
Singapore
www.tierradesign.com

As an early bulwark of capitalism in southeast Asia, Singapore has made money, talent, and ambition coins of the realm. The equatorial island republic's mercantile tradition, dating to colonial days, makes Singapore especially receptive to western tastes and modern styles. The Loft is emblematic of Singapore's embrace of the latest and greatest.

Its neighborhood, Nassim Hill, was the favored residential enclave of the British colonials who used Singapore as a trading outpost until the republic gained independence in 1965. Close to downtown, this area also benefits from a high elevation and sea breezes that temper the tropical climate. Embassies make their home here and Orchard Road, the commercial connector to downtown Singapore, is nearby, making Nassim Hill a convenient residential location.

The Loft's 0.75-hectare (1.85 ac) site became available in 1999 when a three-story hotel ceased operations. The location was ideally suited for luxury housing and the parcel had been zoned for "permanent residential" use, presenting an opportunity to capitalize on the lucrative luxury-housing market. Developer CapitaLand Residential, the residential subsidiary of Singapore-based real estate development giant CapitaLand, knew just what to do to reach the right target market: young, high-net-worth, high-income, cosmopolitan professionals.

Located on the south-facing slope of Nassim Hill, the site is roughly triangular. A green buffer was retained at the periphery of the property to protect ten 100-year-old tembusu trees—a native, endangered,

Project Data

Web Site

www.capitalandresidential.com/
projects/loft

Site Area

0.75 hectares (1.85 ac)

Facilities   77 residential units

Land Uses

luxury condominium apartments

Completion Date   May 2002

Jury Statement

The Loft is a prototype for enlightened development practices brought to bear on a small, hilly, triangular parcel in the desirable Nassim Hill area of Singapore. Natural landscape features in the central courtyard garden, along with the preservation of ten century-old tembusu trees, combine with modern architectural features—innovative glazing and sun-shading systems, glass-enclosed interconnecting bridges, terraces, and granite walls—to soften the density of the 77 residential condominium units.

and protected species—that form a ring around the parcel. Inside the buffer, four-story housing was arranged around a central, green courtyard. This was an efficient way of putting 77 units on a small parcel with maximal open space. The housing units, which are 12 to 16 meters (39 to 52 ft) deep, extend from the outside perimeter through to the courtyard, so that they are cross-ventilated. The bedrooms are placed on the outside perimeter, where visual privacy is achieved by means of solid walls and minimal fenestration. More active living spaces face the courtyard, and courtyard views are assured by means of transparent facades.

The design's synthesis of architectural modernism and vernacular response to the climate is expressed most markedly in a brise soleil that shades the floor-to-ceiling sliding glass walls. The towering tembusus and mature, transplanted willow trees in the courtyard also provide solar shading. A granite-faced retaining wall adds a strong linear element to the courtyard, while concealing part of the two-story parking garage and addressing the changes in level on the hillside site. The vertical wall is punctuated with rectangular crevices in which Kyoto grass grows. A 25-meter-long (82 ft) swimming pool is located on the lower terrace.

Numerous openings between the building blocks allow breezes to flow through the site and provide views. The one- to three-bedroom condominium units range in size from 70 to 174 square meters (753 to 1,873 sf). All units have been sold. Among the sold units, 60 percent are being leased by investors at rates ranging between s$40.36 and s$52.20 per square meter (US$2.25 and US$2.90 per sf) per month, compared with the Singapore average rental rate for prime apartments of s$24.76 per square meter (US$1.38 per sf).

MEANDER

Amsterdam, The Netherlands

Het Oosten Kristal and Latei are two Dutch not-for-profit developers of low-cost housing who combined forces to create Meander, a vibrant mixed-use community, in a location where for more than two decades the city had been trying—unsuccessfully—to jump-start development. On paper, the 1.7-hectare (4.2 ac) site seemed to offer a ripe opportunity: canal frontage, close to downtown (2.5 kilometers or 1.6 miles west), and high on the list of sites that the city was eager to see developed. Until the context was revealed: The site was in Westerpark.

To the people of Amsterdam, Westerpark signifies squatters. Once associated with political activism, squatting is legally protected to an extent, but essentially it has devolved into an alternative to homelessness. The city borough of Westerpark (population 34,000) is especially attractive to squatters because of its proximity to downtown and because it is pocked with abandoned industrial buildings. Various tactics, including the condemnation and even demolition of targeted buildings, have been used to oust the squatters, but the squatter population has been resilient.

Although the Westerpark borough government had targeted this site on Kostverlorenvaart, an inland shipping canal, for redevelopment, progress on a succession of proposals was stalled by a combination of squatters exercising their legal rights and the developer's inability to project profits under such a muddled situation.

Still, some small housing developments elsewhere in this immediate neighborhood had been started and piecemeal gentrification was beginning to transform Westerpark. Given this environment, Het Oosten Kristal and Latei thought that a high-density residential community that received government funding for public and nonprofit uses—such as a library, school facilities, and artist studios—could be financially successful. The borough government approved the development team's proposal to increase the project's density and to reduce the number of affordable apartments that would be required in return for setting aside space for an elementary school and a branch of the public library, giving the developers leverage to obtain private funding.

The master plan revolves around two internal streets that open as a V to the canal. They are lined with five-story apartment buildings in an arrangement that maximizes the number of apartments with views to the canal, thus maximizing the rent revenue. Three cylindrical, seven-story blocks contain apartments that offer panoramic views of the water and act as pivots for the housing rows. The affordable units are located on the backside of this meandering shape and they face a sinuous courtyard. Townhouses line the external streets at the periphery of the site. A wide plazalike promenade that is paved in stone and brick runs along the canal and provides public access to the water's edge.

Development Team

Owners/Developers

**Het Oosten Kristal
Amsterdam, The Netherlands
www.hetoosten.nl**

**Latei
Amersfoort, The Netherlands
www.latei.nl**

Architect

**Rob Krier/Cristoph Kohl
Berlin, Germany
www.krierkohl.com**

Project Data

Web Site **www.meanderwonen.nl**

Site Area **1.7 hectares (4.2 ac)**

Facilities

50,366 square meters (542,135 sf) gross building area

41,749 square meters (460,146 sf) gross leasable area

276 rental apartments

240 parking spaces

Land Uses **housing, retail, community facilities, artist studios, parking, public access to canal**

Completion Dates

2001 for Phase 1

2005 for Phase 2

Jury Statement

This 1.7-hectare (4.2 ac) housing development has converted derelict canalfront land encumbered by squatter housing into a mixed-use, mixed-income community with 276 rental apartments. Named after the way the new housing complex winds (meanders) along the canal, Meander provides ample parking in an area lacking it, opens public access to the canal, and features a diversity of community facilities—including a primary school, a public library, a restaurant, and studios targeted to beginning artists.

With 160 units per hectare (65 per ac), Meander is one of the highest-density modern residential developments in Amsterdam. It contains 276 housing units and 1,454 square meters (15,651 sf) of leasable commercial space. Most of the commercial space is occupied by a ground-floor restaurant facing the canal that has become a popular, even trendy, spot with customers from throughout Amsterdam. The second phase of Meander, now nearing completion, will provide the not-for-profit Phase 2 uses—a primary school and a public library together occupying 1,773 square meters (19,084 sf) and 455 square meters (4,900 sf) of studio space designated for beginning artists.

THE PARK LAUREL

New York, New York

Development Team

Owner

VNO 63rd Street, LLC
New York, New York

Developer

Vornado Realty Trust
New York, New York
www.vno.com

Architects

Beyer Blinder Belle Architects
New York, New York
www.beyerblinderbelle.com

Costas Kondylis & Partners
New York, New York
www.kondylis.com

Project Data

Site Area **7,897 square feet (734 m)**

Facilities

213,000 square feet (19,788 m²) gross building area

119,000 square feet (11,055 m²) net salable area

53 luxury condominium apartments; 67 affordable housing units

Land Uses

luxury condominiums; YMCA classroom, exercise, and SRO facilities

Completion Date **March 2003**

The Park Laurel is a 41-story luxury residential condominium tower constructed next to and above the landmark West Side YMCA on West 63rd Street overlooking Central Park in Manhattan. The air-rights development added 53 luxury condominiums in a desirable neighborhood, expanded and rehabilitated a historic community facility (the YMCA), preserved the facade of a historic school (McBurney School), and created 67 affordable housing units.

The YMCA first conceived a plan to capitalize on the value of its real estate in the mid-1980s. It would sell the adjacent five-story McBurney School property plus air rights above the landmark YMCA building for the development of a luxury residential condominium tower, and use the profits to expand its facilities and programs as well as fund needed capital improvements. The initial attempt at development was sidelined by a real estate recession. In 1997, the YMCA resurrected its plans, and after 18 months of negotiations sold its air rights to a development entity established by New York–based Vornado Realty Trust.

The YMCA received cash to improve its existing building, ownership of the 11 lower stories of the new building that it uses for program space and 67 single-room-occupancy (SRO) units, and a share of the profits on the condominium sales. The prewar-style condominiums developed by Vornado occupy floors 12 through 40, with the penthouse being a duplex. Based solely on floor plans and marketing materials, 98 percent of the condominiums were presold at prices that were above projections.

Many complex challenges arose throughout the approval, design, and development processes. Strict guidelines set by the city's landmarks preservation and planning commissions required designing within a nonnegotiable, preapproved building envelope that included height limitations at various setbacks, and protection of the YMCA building during construction. The school's historic 1931 facade was incorporated as the entrance to the Park Laurel condominiums, and the top 26 stories of the new tower were cantilevered over the YMCA building.

Participation in the city's inclusionary housing program increased the project's floor/area ratio (FAR) from 10 to 12 and gained the developer an additional 70,000 square feet (6,503 m²) of area, 20,000 square feet (1,858 m²) of which was given over to affordable housing. The project also qualified for a partial exemption from real estate taxes for ten years under the city's 421(a) program for projects providing multifamily units on vacant or underutilized lots and affordable housing.

Built on a complicated infill site, the Park Laurel took advantage of a great location and provided the means for a landmark community facility—the West Side YMCA—to modernize and expand while maintaining the historic character of its original building. High-quality planning and sensitive design have assured that the old and new buildings complement each other on the site.

PIER 6/7, WALSH BAY

Sydney, Australia

Even if this luxury condominium building were built on land, it—and the Walsh Bay revitalization going on around it—would be marked as a special development. That the environmentally aware residential structure incorporating both car parking and boat slips was built over water marks it as extraordinary and innovative. Imagine a 200-by-24-meter (656×79 ft), seven-story multifamily building atop the typical below-grade parking towed out to the harbor and anchored on pilings—a fair approximation of Pier 6/7's concept.

The ongoing redevelopment of Sydney's Walsh Bay is the southern hemisphere's largest urban renewal project by a single entity, and Pier 6/7 is its crown jewel. After a decade of seeking to involve private developers in the revitalization of the 17-hectare (42 ac) Walsh Bay historic district, a dilapidated harbor precinct of timber, stone, and brick structures adjacent to Sydney Harbour Bridge, the New South Wales government finally awarded development rights in 1995 to a Mirvac/Transfield joint venture under a 99-year leasehold. (The 99-year lease periods commence with the completion of each building.)

The winning proposal was based on a redevelopment plan incorporating a mix of residential, commercial, and recreational uses; renovation and new development; and public access to the waterfront. The plan's attention to historic and environmental preservation helped make it acceptable. After negotiations with more than 40 stakeholders—government agencies and citizen groups—the development partnership successfully lobbied the government to obtain a parliamentary act that ensured government approval of the master plan, thus negating the risk of future court challenges.

The bayshore area of the Walsh Bay historic precinct features a half-kilometer-long (one-third mile) promenade along which stretch 457 square meters (4,919 sf) of retail and 594 square meters (6,394 sf) of cultural facilities at promenade level with 3,500 square meters (37,675 sf) of office space and 99 residential units above. The inland blocks contain more office, residential, and retail space interspersed with parks and public plazas, with much space on the upper levels having harbor views. In all, the precinct currently contains 17 new and refurbished buildings totaling approximately 200,000 square meters (2.1 million sf) of space. Pier 6/7 is one of four finger piers, and the only one with a residential component.

Pier 6/7 is the architectural and development centerpiece of the Walsh Bay precinct. Largely because of historic preservation regulations that confined the footprint to that of the original pier, the building's design resembles a boat with its shallow bargelike "hull" containing a below-deck level of parking. The building, which sits on the deck, contains back-to-back duplex units on the bottom, each with its own internal stairs; topped by three stories of through-units having views on both sides of the pier; topped by a penthouse level with 32 duplex units.

Development Team

Owners/Developers

**Walsh Bay Partnership
(Mirvac/Transfield joint venture)**

**Mirvac Group
North Sydney, Australia
www.mirvac.com.au**

**Transfield Holdings Pty, Ltd.
Sydney, Australia
www.transfield.com.au**

Architects

**HPA
Sydney, Australia
www.mirvac.com.au**

**PTW
Sydney, Australia
www.ptw.com.au**

Project Data

Web Site **www.mirvac.com.au**

Site Area **9,484 m² (102,085 sf)**

Facilities

42,000 m² (452,100 sf) total building area

140 residential units

387 parking spaces

49 boat slips

Land Uses

multifamily residential, recreational

Completion Date **March 2003**

Jury Statement

In Sydney's Walsh Bay, within the footprint of the former finger wharf number 6/7, the development partnership built 140 luxury condominiums, 387 parking spaces under the waterline, and 49 boat moorings. The complex—the only known pier in the world purpose-built for this use—is the crown jewel of the entire Walsh Bay development district and is a model for creative reuse of the waterfront.

Forty-nine moving pontoons on the deck level are available for ownership, with Pier 6/7 residents given preference. The 387 parking spaces below deck are reserved for residents and boat-slip users.

Pier 6/7 is designed for minimal maintenance over the 99-year lease term. Forms for the concrete "hull" were constructed on land, floated into place, and attached to hollow steel piers driven 50 meters (164 ft) below the waterline. After the concrete was poured, the slab was jacked down below water level— a procedure never before attempted—and anchored to the concrete-filled piers. Custom-designed, motorized, 200-millimeter-wide (8 in) louvers protect the building from sun, glare, salt, and wind. Steel components are marine-grade anodized stainless steel.

All 140 units sold within ten days of Pier 6/7's sales launch in March 2000, at asking prices between AU$1 million and AU$5.8 million (US$620,000 and US$3.6 million). Subsequent resale prices reflect an average increase in value of 23 percent.

Even without Pier 6/7, Walsh Bay can be considered a successful development from any point of view. All its bayfront condominiums sold out as soon as they became available, and except for some of the retail space that has been leased but not yet fitted out, the entire development is at full occupancy. With Pier 6/7, Walsh Bay takes mixed-use harborfront development to a new level of accomplishment.

WOONHAVEN 'T ZANDRAK

Capelle aan den IJssel, The Netherlands

Development Team

Owner/Developer

AM Wonen
Nieuwegein, The Netherlands
www.amwonen.nl

Architects

Atelier Kingma & Van Mameren
Schiedam, The Netherlands
www.atelierkvm.nl

1–10 Architecten
Rotterdam, The Netherlands
www.eentien.nl

Schippers Architecten
The Hague, The Netherlands
www.schippers-bna.nl

As every schoolchild knows, two-thirds of Holland would be under water if it were not for dikes. Constructed dikes, not natural shorelines, define the water's edge in the inland parts of the Netherlands. Inside the dike, habitation occurs; outside the dike, there is only water. In this context, the development of Woonhaven 't Zandrak ("built outside the dike" in English) makes it unique and "outside the box" in more ways than one.

AM Wonen, the residential development arm of the giant AM real estate company, seized on the opportunity to transform a failing, run-down, and polluted marina on the Hollandse IJssel river into a residential yachting marina with impossible-to-match views of the water. The first task was to clean up the riverbanks—a worthwhile undertaking in itself—and reclaim riverbank land.

Some of the site's solid waste stemmed from the operations of a former municipal waste facility, which had used water from the river to rinse waste before carting it away to a landfill. The marina that succeeded the waste facility had further polluted the area with motor-oil sludge from power boats and leakage from fuel-storage tanks. In consultation with local and national governments, AM Wonen reclaimed some land by erecting sheet pile walls and excavating river bank from the IJssel, and brought in topsoil for a clean finished layer. The resulting land area—about 5.5 hectares (13.6 ac)—would be just enough to build enough houses to justify the cost of the land reclamation and environmental restoration work. Land acquisition proceeded during the three years it took to complete the reclamation work. Purchasing the marina was the easy part. Purchasing the marina's many long-term houseboat leases was harder, requiring luck and perseverance.

Various municipal authorities needed assurance that Zandrak would be a responsible caretaker of the land and water resources that AM Wonen was restoring. With this in mind, the developer established a pilot riverbank cleanup program involving a number of public sector agencies—the water authority; the public works and water management directorate; the environmental protection agency; and the housing, planning, and environment ministry—and various municipalities. This initiative not only helped to extend the cleanup campaign beyond the boundaries of the project, but also afforded AM Wonen the experience it later needed to tackle other public interfaces involving the management of site-generated water and waste; the defense of the dike; the public use of open spaces; the maintenance of riparian rights, privileges, and responsibilities; and so forth. The developer's tackling of the riverbank cleanup and management issue as an areawide problem enabled AM Wonen to influence such public undertakings as the elimination of a nearby riverside refuse dump and the creation of a river-oriented nature preserve on adjacent land.

Zandrak is designed to give all house lots a river view and a sunny yard. Its market-driven mix of 103 detached and attached single-family houses range in price from €350,000 to €750,000 ($463,540 to $993,300). A seven-story, 28-unit apartment building forms a prow—acting as a landmark for river users—on a point of land where the IJssel bends around the site. Seven of its units are still available at prices ranging from €452,500 to €610,000 ($599,291 to $807,884). A 2.1-hectare (5.1 ac) marina has 115 berths, which are offered first to homeowners in Zandrak before they are sold to the public. (Zandrak is one of the few places in metropolitan Rotterdam that offers for-sale boat slips.)

Construction and sales have kept pace with the enormous costs incurred in land reclamation, environmental restoration, and mitigation, but buildout took four years. AM Wonen reports that Zandrak's overall financial performance has been above standard. Not that this concerns the residents of Zandrak, who are inclined to believe that the price premium they paid for living outside the dike—with sweeping views of the newly cleaned-up river—was well worth it.

Project Data

Web Site **www.zandrak.nl**

Site Area

5.5 hectares (13.6 ac) total site area

2.1 hectares (5.1 ac) marina area

Facilities

55,000 square meters (592,034 sf) total building area

131 residential units: 103 single-family houses, 28 for-sale apartments

Land Uses **residential, marina**

Completion Date **2005**

NEW COMMUNITY

THE GLEN

Glenview, Illinois

More than just an example of the successful redevelopment and integration of a closed military base with its community, The Glen is also a textbook example of how a town can build consensus among its citizens and marshal its resources to obtain the best outcome for a challenging real estate opportunity.

In 1993, the U.S. Department of Defense announced the scheduled closure of the Glenview Naval Air Station, a busy training site during World War II, but more recently used to train reservists. The Village of Glenview decided to act as the redevelopment authority to ensure the smooth transfer of the site from military to general use. Soon after the closure was announced, the village began an 18-month process to put together a comprehensive business and operational plan that served as the basis for a no-cost transfer of the property in 1997.

Three factors favored this base redevelopment project: (1) the entire base was within Glenview's jurisdiction; (2) Glenview was an affluent North Shore suburb of Chicago with a median household income above $100,000; and (3) the number of civilians working at the base was less than 400, so the closure had minimal economic consequences. Base conversions are often crippled by interjurisdictional complexities, weak markets, or the adverse impacts of closure on the local economy.

Working with Mesirow Stein Real Estate as development adviser and Skidmore, Owings & Merrill as master planner, the Village of Glenview decided on a mixed-use plan that would seamlessly integrate the redeveloped Glen into the town. The master plan had five goals: a mixed-use town center, walkable neighborhoods, a connected street system, connected open spaces, and the flexibility to accommodate growth.

The Glen Town Center, a $150 million lifestyle center, contains 470,000 square feet (43,663 m²) of retail and commercial space, with 181 rental apartments on the upper stories. A historic hangar that is listed on the national landmark registry has been converted into retail space. On the periphery of the town center there are 154 for-sale townhouses. Surrounding the town center is a 140-acre (58 ha) park, the Kohl Children's Museum, and two golf courses.

Seeking to balance its revenues from land sales with the cost of the infrastructure and public services needed to support new development, the Village of Glenview opted for less density and more open space. Almost 40 percent of the land area of The Glen is public open space, and a considerable amount of land sculpting was undertaken to create amenities on the flat former airfield. One million cubic yards (764,555 m³) of earth was removed to create Lake Glenview, a stormwater detention facility that is also a recreational amenity. Nearly 450,000 cubic yards (344,050 m³) of concrete from the airfield's 1.5 miles (2.4 km) of runways was stored and crushed on site; much of it was sold off or reused on site for new roadway and utility corridors. The navy spent $25 million on site remediation.

Development Team

Owner/Developer
The Village of Glenview
www.glenview.il.us

Development Adviser
Mesirow Stein Real Estate, Inc.
Chicago, Illinois
www.mesirowfinancial.com

Planner
Skidmore, Owings & Merrill
Chicago, Illinois
www.som.com

The Village of Glenview's $477 million in expenditures on infrastructure, incentives, and interest will be funded from approximately $800 million in revenue from grants, land sales, and property taxes. Interim financing for the project was provided by $145 million in general obligation bonds from the Village of Glenview. The Glen is substantially complete, with an estimated value of $1.1 billion. The project will add 5,000 new residents, contribute 5,000 full-time jobs, and increase the local tax base by 35 percent. The Village of Glenview assumed a measured risk in acting as its own redevelopment authority, but it has succeeded in selling the land—and development will soon make Glenview a whole town.

Project Data

Web Site www.glenview.il.us/glen

Site Area

1,121 acres (454 ha) total site area

88 acres (36 ha) business park area

84 acres (34 ha) retail/commercial area

342 acres (138 ha) total residential area; including 38 acres (15 ha) seniors' housing area

418 acres (169 ha) parks and open space

219 acres (89 ha) golf

105 acres (42 ha) public service area

Facilities

1,033,414 square feet (96,004 m²) business park space

925,200 square feet (85,951 m²) retail space

1,969 total housing units: 567 single-family units, 729 multifamily units, 673 seniors' units

Land Uses residential, business park, golf, retail, open space, and parks

Completion Date

as of mid-2005, 95 percent of land sales are complete

Jury Statement

The closure of the Glenview Naval Air Station provided an opportunity for the Village of Glenview to integrate the base's 1,121 acres (454 ha) into the town's context while dedicating almost 40 percent of the site to public use. The mixed-use development, now known as The Glen, is an integral part of the town, and a model for dozens of future base closings.

NEW COMMUNITY · WINNER

HARBOR TOWN

Memphis, Tennessee

Harbor Town, finished in 2004 after a 15-year development period, is one of the earliest examples of a traditional neighborhood development (TND) and certainly one of the most complete. It is located on Mud Island, a 400-acre (162 ha), two-mile-long peninsula on the Memphis side of the Mississippi River. The development site was a barren vacant parcel adjacent to Memphis's central business district, but miles away from any housing less than 100 years old. Its design—gridded streets, many terminating in small parks; wide radial boulevards; a strong pedestrian orientation; formally planned public squares; and architectural forms based on historical prototypes—embodies many of the basic principles of TND.

The dream of Memphis-based developer Henry M. Turley, Jr., was to re-create the spirit of the old Memphis neighborhood where he grew up, a neighborhood with a mix of rich and poor residents, and a few small shops and other businesses where people met and developed friendships. "Right there in my neighborhood," he recalls, "there seemed to be everything—a hint of all of life's possibilities mixed with all kinds of people." In Harbor Town, Turley sought to establish a similar neighborhood ethos and sense of community, and thus do his part to challenge the market's fear of cities, diversity, and minorities that was driving suburban sprawl development east of Memphis. With the help of two local developers, Jack Belz and Meredith L. McCullar, private financing was obtained for the entire project, making it possible to circumvent certain planning and zoning regulations that would have posed obstacles to the TND design.

The master plan, originally designed by RTKL Associates and later taken over by Looney Ricks Kiss (LRK), incorporates three distinct, yet interconnected neighborhoods—garden district, village district, and harbor district. A wetlands retention feature designed to look like a stream and ponds runs through the center of the site, creating a natural boundary between neighborhoods.

The centrally located garden district contains a mix of townhouses, zero-lot-line detached houses, and larger detached houses. The village district, which is located on the north, is the most densely configured neighborhood. It contains rental apartments and a variety of for-sale detached, courtyard houses. The harbor district on the south end features the town square, which is fashioned after a traditional small-town main street and around which are found a bilingual daycare center, a Montessori school, 42 rental apartments (located above retail stores), restaurants, professional offices, and a 5,800-square-foot (539 m²) grocery store.

The provision of a broad mix of housing types, sizes, styles, and price ranges is a central element in the Harbor Town concept. The project's inclusion of a wide range of price points broke every known pricing guideline. Units renting for $800 a month are located just a few steps from $800,000 riverfront houses. Single-family houses range from 1,000 to 6,000 square feet (93 to 557 m²), and some are production-built

Development Team

Owners/Developers

Henry Turley Company
Memphis, Tennessee
www.henryturley.com

Belz Enterprises
Memphis, Tennessee
www.belz.com

Master Planner and Town Architect

Looney Ricks Kiss Architects
Memphis, Tennessee
www.lrk.com

Master Planner (original plan)

RTKL Associates, Inc.
Baltimore, Maryland
www.rtkl.com

Consultant

Bologna Consultants
Memphis, Tennessee

Landscape Architect

Reaves & Sweeney
Memphis, Tennessee

Project Data

Web Site

www.henryturley.com/homes

Site Area **135 acres (54.6 ha)**

Facilities

30,000 square feet (2,787 m²) office space

25,000 square feet (2,323 m²) retail space

1,000 residential units: 421 rental units, 122 for-sale townhouses, 457 for-sale detached houses

Land Uses

residential, mixed-use town center with rental apartments above retail, elementary school, marina, inn

Completion Date **2004**

Jury Statement

A pioneering new community, Harbor Town broke all the rules when it started out in 1989. The 135-acre (54.6 ha), mixed-use community on a Mississippi River peninsula mixes a wide variety of housing types with a diversity of price points, emerging as one of the most cited early examples of a primary-home traditional neighborhood development.

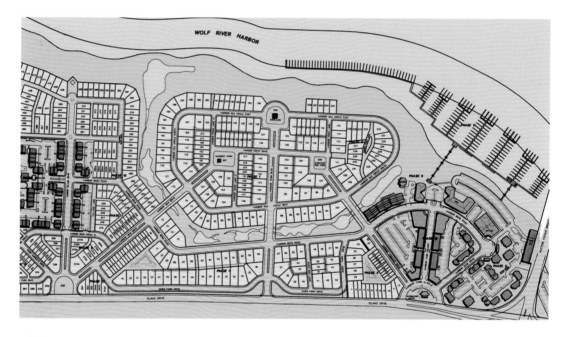

while others are custom-built. Harbor Town's housing diversity is matched by demographic diversity, and the project has attracted many empty nesters, singles, and professional couples.

Most of the residential designs are updated version of such vernacular styles as Charleston sideyard houses, simple shotgun cottages, and dog-trot houses. Visual design guidelines—created by LRK in a format that has become the standard in the industry—were established to translate the TND vision into dos and don'ts, but particular architectural styles are not prescribed. The intent of the guidelines is to create an overall aesthetic for the community and ensure that lower-price housing maintains a level of design compatible in quality to the most expensive houses.

The average house sale price in 1991, the year that sales began, was $187,995; in 2004, it was $368,348. Resale price escalation has been equally dramatic, with one house selling in 1996 for $262,000, in 2002 for $365,000, and in 2004 for $445,000. Ultimately, however, Harbor Town's success is better measured in nonfinancial terms: The development has attracted a diversity of residents, customers, visitors, and workers back to downtown Memphis and the market success of Harbor Town has spurred the development of other TND-style alternatives to suburban living within the city of Memphis and around the region.

HARVEST LAKES

Perth, Australia

Development Team

Owner/Developer

LandCorp
Perth, Australia
www.landcorp.com.au

Planner

Roberts Day Group
East Perth, Australia
www.robertsday.com.au

Landscape Architect

McNally Newton
Northbridge, Australia
www.mnla.com.au

Architect

Sharni Howe Architects
Perth, Australia

Project Manager

Benchmark Projects
East Perth, Australia
www.benchmarkprojects.com.au

Project Data

Web Site **www.harvestlakes.com.au**

Site Area **115 hectares (284 ac)**

Land Uses **residential (1,000 lots),**
community facilities

Completion Date **2008**

Harvest Lakes, which is transforming 115 hectares (284 ac) of degraded former farmland into a sustainable community for 1,000 households, is an emerging model for residential greenfield development—for Australia, as well as for countries around the globe. This living experiment involves the major participants in the state of Western Australia's smart growth movement, who are seeking to demonstrate how an integrated collection of achievable community-building, housing, and neighborhood-design initiatives can result in environmentally and financially sound residential development.

Located 23 kilometers (14 mi) and 20 minutes by freeway from the state's capital city of Perth in the region's rapidly growing southwest corridor, Harvest Lakes is served by an interchange of the Kwinana Freeway and is a planned location for a station on the future Perth/Mandurah commuter-rail line. In partnership with various political jurisdictions and public sector infrastructure providers, LandCorp, an agency operated by the state government, is developing the land. As LandCorp's role in Harvest Lakes winds down, the private side of this public/private partnership—the 14 homebuilders who are building the housing—and the local government will control more of the development.

The Roberts Day Group's master plan incorporates many traditional neighborhood design (TND) principles, such as mandatory architectural design guidelines, a focus on passive design techniques to conserve energy, walkability, and open street layout that enhances security—without attempting to achieve the high density and income mix for which new urbanist plans aim.

Environmental protection is the defining characteristic of the development and a major draw in attracting buyers. In addition to its energy-conserving design guidelines—such as maximal winter solar orientation and maximal summer shading, siting and other passive means of harnessing natural breezes, and landscape elements that stabilize temperatures inside the houses—Harvest Lakes has a strong water management plan. Two threatened wetland areas have been restored—one as a swimmable lake and the other as a seasonal wetland—providing havens for wildlife and native flora. Most important, the restored wetlands are integrated with the stormwater management system. Stormwater is harvested and mixed with well water to maintain public recreation areas and recharge the underground aquifer with 135,000 kiloliters (35.7 million gal) annually. Financial incentives are in place to encourage residents to maintain the water-efficient gardens that are required by the development's landscaping guidelines.

LandCorp has provided Harvest Lakes with a number of community facilities that have been designed and built to sustainability criteria. These include a primary school—which is the first in the state to be built to strict criteria—and the first purpose-built community center in the country designed to Australia's ecologically sustainable design (ESD) principles.

Harvest Lakes outsells all residential developments in Perth's southwest corridor. Phased lot sales opened in November 2002, and each phase has sold out within a week. Many would-be purchasers have camped out for up to three weeks to secure their preferred lot, drawing widespread media coverage. Land prices have doubled since the first lots went on sale.

Halfway toward buildout, Harvest Lakes already illustrates how suburban residential development can incorporate significant environmental features without being unprofitable for the developer or unaffordable for homebuyers. LandCorp CEO Ross Holt says that "a sustainable development should be not only buildable, but also bankable." Harvest Lakes is maintaining a balance of buildability and bankability—and raising the profile of environmental sustainability issues in Australia. Harvest Lakes is the first—and largest—land development in Western Australia to receive the Housing Industry Association of Australia's "GreenSmart" accreditation.

PRAIRIE CROSSING

Grayslake, Illinois

Development Team

Owner/Developer

Prairie Holdings Corporation
Grayslake, Illinois
www.prairiecrossing.com

Development Manager
(initial stages)

The Shaw Companies
Chicago, Illinois
www.shaw-co.com

Land Planners

Skidmore, Owings & Merrill
Chicago, Illinois
www.som.com

Calthorpe Associates
Berkeley, California
www.calthorpe.com

Landscape Architects

William Johnson, FASLA
Bainbridge Island, Washington

Peter Lindsay Schaudt Landscape
Architecture, Inc.
Chicago, Illinois
www.schaudt.ws

Architects

Worn Jerabek Architects
Chicago, Illinois
www.wwapc.com

Serena Sturm Architects
Northbrook, Illinois
www.serenasturm.com

Prairie Crossing is a pioneer "conservation development." The project demonstrates how ecologically sensitive development can be used as a tool for the conservation of land that is threatened by inappropriate land uses. The development of Prairie Crossing adhered to a set of founding principles and serves as a model for sustainable land development.

The 678-acre (274 ha) site was farmland located 45 miles (72 km) north of Chicago. In 1987, after a 15-year battle over its development, Gaylord Donnelley, a Chicago printing executive who lived nearby, and seven neighboring families formed Prairie Holdings Corporation (PHC) to purchase and control the land.

Under a 1986 legal settlement, the tract had been permitted to be developed as a typical subdivision with 1,600 houses. The new owner set out to create a profitable new community that would leave as much land as feasible in a natural or agricultural condition by clustering houses on smaller-than-conventional lots. In essence, homebuyers would be trading off private acreage for shared ownership of open space.

PHC established ten principles of conservation development for Prairie Crossing: (1) environmental protection and enhancement; (2) a healthy lifestyle; (3) a sense of place; (4) a sense of community; (5) economic and racial diversity; (6) convenient and efficient transportation options; (7) energy conservation; (8) lifelong learning and education; (9) aesthetic design and high-quality construction; and (10) economic viability.

More than two-thirds of the site—470 acres (190 ha)—is protected from development by covenant. Development is located to protect the most valuable native vegetation and other environmental assets, and most houses feature long views over open land. Prairie Crossing's greenways are part of the Liberty Prairie Reserve, a 5,800-acre (2,347 ha) collection of public and private landholdings that includes nature preserves, forest preserves, farms, and trails. Prairie Crossing proper contains more than ten miles (16 km) of trails, a stable, a recreational lake that holds stormwater purified by passage through restored prairies and wetlands, and a 90-acre (36 ha) organic farm.

The houses have been constructed with materials and techniques that reduce energy consumption by approximately 50 percent compared with other new houses in the area. A wind turbine provides power to the farm. The charter school building meets Leadership in Energy and Environmental Design (LEED) standards—while the school itself offers elementary education based on an environmental curriculum. Informal education programs on environmental subjects are offered by the Liberty Prairie Conservancy, the Prairie Crossing Institute, and the Learning Farm at the organic farm.

Community-wide recycling and composting programs are in effect. The design of the community encourages residents to walk or bike rather than drive to nearby destinations. Trails connect Prairie Crossing

Project Data

Web Site **www.prairiecrossing.com**

Site Area **678 acres (274 ha)**

Facilities

**20,000 square feet (1,858 m²)
office space**

**52,500 square feet (4,877 m²)
retail space**

**395 residential units: 359 single-family
detached units, 36 condominiums**

Land Uses **residential, mixed commercial/educational/civic, farmland,
open space**

Completion Date **2006**

to such neighboring destinations as two train stations providing rail service to Chicago (one hour away) and O'Hare Airport, two regional centers of higher education, a public high school, the Liberty Prairie Reserve, and local stores and restaurants. Station Square, a mixed-use neighborhood of shops, restaurants, and residential condominiums anchored by a commuter-rail station, currently is under development.

The last of Prairie Crossing's 359 single-family houses sold in 2005, with initial prices ranging from $179,900 to well over $500,000, an estimated 33 percent premium per square foot above comparable houses in the area. A covenant provides 0.5 percent of the sale price of each house to the Liberty Prairie Foundation, which supports environmental programs at Prairie Crossing and beyond.

PUEBLO DEL SOL

Los Angeles, California

HOPE VI (Housing Opportunities for People Everywhere) projects are not for the faint of heart. Their developers must orchestrate multiple financing options, balance competing jurisdictional demands, and design affordable housing that does not look "affordable." Pueblo del Sol shows how to use the HOPE VI apparatus to rejuvenate inner-city residential neighborhoods.

The new Pueblo del Sol, containing 377 rental apartments and 93 for-sale attached houses, replaces a 685-unit public housing project, Aliso Village, that was built in 1942 and condemned in 1998. It was not so much that the buildings were structurally unsound, as that uncontrollable drug gangs made them unsafe. Located in predominantly Latino East Los Angeles, Aliso Village was part of Pico Aliso—the largest public housing complex west of the Mississippi and home to 11 active street gangs.

Sponsored by the U.S. Department of Housing and Urban Development (HUD), the HOPE VI program replaces public housing with privately developed housing that meets HUD guidelines for affordability. Typically, one-fourth of a project's units must be reserved for households with incomes below 25 percent of the area median, one-fourth for households between 25 and 50 percent of the median, and the remaining units for households up to 115 percent of the median. HUD provides a grant to cover a project's capital costs, with the proviso that the grant be used to leverage private investment. The families that were displaced from the public housing receive priority in the rental or purchase of the new units. (Displaced households can use Section 8 vouchers to find temporary—or permanent—housing elsewhere.) And the residents and managers of the replacement housing are empowered to enforce a zero-tolerance policy of responsible behavior within the premises.

The Housing Authority of the City of Los Angeles (HACLA) brought the 29-acre (11.7 ha) site (which is leased from the city of Los Angeles) and a $30 million HUD grant to the partnership. The selected joint venture partner—the Related Companies of California—contributed development expertise and leveraged the public money to gain another $90 million in private sector financing.

HOPE VI has new urbanist roots that are reflected in its goal of mixed-income, neighborly, and safe communities. At Pueblo del Sol, density is high—up to 22.5 housing units per acre (56 per ha). Private patios and decks face the public streets and courtyards, in order to keep many "eyes on the street." On-street parallel parking keeps parking lots to a minimum. Vehicular through circulation is unavailable, minimizing the potential for drive-by shootings. And 90 percent of the apartments feature attached one-car garages.

The first phase of the rental units, which range from 900 to 1,200 square feet (84 to 111 m²), came on line in December 2003. Since then, Pueblo del Sol has remained fully leased up and the waiting list has grown to 2,000. The rental units are targeted to households with incomes from 30 to 60 percent of

Development Team

Owners/Developers

The Related Companies of California
Irvine, California
www.related.com

McCormack Baron Salazar
(marketing of rental housing)
St. Louis, Missouri
www.mba-development.com

The Lee Group (marketing of
for-sale housing)
Los Angeles, California

Public Partner

**Housing Authority of the City of
Los Angeles**
www.hacla.org

Planners/Architects

Quatro Design Group
Los Angeles, California
www.qdg-architects.com

Wraight Architects
Irvine, California

William Hezmalhalch Architects, Inc.
Santa Ana, California
www.whainc.com

Van Tilburg, Banvard & Soderbergh
Santa Monica, California
www.vtbs.com

the median income in Los Angeles County. The three- and four-bedroom for-sale townhouses came on line in April 2005, and all were presold—by lottery, because so many people were interested, and at market rate.

A preexisting elementary school is located at the center of the project. Other community facilities include a 1.5-acre (0.6 ha) park, two new community centers, a public swimming pool, and numerous tot-lots. An MTA light-rail station is under construction and a future phase that will include a supermarket and street-oriented retail is planned, as is a magnet high school.

Pueblo del Sol provides a fiscally viable and socially responsive new community that resolves many of the issues that can doom publicly subsidized housing to failure. It is a mixed-use, shared-use, and mixed-income neighborhood that has attracted a diverse population. The residential neighborhood is walkable, connected to transit, linked to existing street patterns, and secure—without the use of gates and barriers.

Project Data

Web Site **www.related.com**

Site Area **29 acres (11.7 ha)**

Facilities

13,000 square feet (1,208 m²) gross non-residential building area

470 housing units: 377 rental units, 93 for-sale units

Land Uses

housing, park, community facilities

Completion Date **2005**

Jury Statement

Formerly a public housing project known as Aliso Village—a home to street gangs as well as 800 obsolete units—the 29-acre (11.7 ha) parcel today provides 377 rental and 93 for-sale units. This HOPE VI project not only has resurrected itself, but also has revitalized its entire community as the catalyst for a new transit stop, a renovated elementary school, a new community center, and plans for a new high school.

SANTALUZ

San Diego, California

Development Team

Owners/Developers

DMB Associates, Inc.
Scottsdale, Arizona
www.dmbinc.com

Taylor Woodrow Homes
Irvine, California
www.taylorwoodrow.com

Land Planner

SWA Group
Laguna Beach, California
www.swagroup.com

Architect

Robert Hidey Architects
Irvine, California
www.roberthidey.com

Clubhouse Architect

Mason Architecture & Design, Inc.
Denver, Colorado
www.madarch.com

Landscape Architects

Wimmer, Yamada & Caughey
San Diego, California
www.wyac.com

Gillespie Design Group, Inc.
La Jolla, California
www.gillespiedesign.com

Golf Course Architect

Rees Jones, Inc.
Montclair, New Jersey
www.reesjonesinc.com

The Santaluz development team launched this project with a risky decision. It would *not* develop the 3,800-acre (1,537 ha) site as a traditional master-planned community. In the team's view, there was untapped potential in the original, approved plan for what was one of the last large undeveloped parcels in southern California. DMB Associates and Taylor Woodrow Homes decided instead to develop a community inspired by California's early heritage.

The name Santaluz means "sacred light" and the gated community is 30 miles (48 km) north of downtown San Diego. The community was developed under an innovative, low-density land plan that works with the natural terrain and uses natural landscaping; and it features creative architecture, a high level of recreational assets, and attention to detail that together have helped it outperform more typical heavily graded, high-density communities. In addition to 836 homesites, Santaluz comprises an 11-acre (4.5 ha) village green, a 19,000-square-foot (1,765 m²) indoor recreation center, and an 18-hole Rees Jones golf course with a 35,000-square-foot (3,252 m²) clubhouse and spa.

The "big idea" at Santaluz is circular homesite pads that are set close to the natural grade and blend easily into the terrain. Circular lots allow houses to be oriented in any direction to capture views and breezes, and to spread out in long, low wings for optimal indoor/outdoor living. They also require only half the earthwork of traditional grading. "Circular homesites like this had never been developed before," says Dick Law, principal, SWA Group. "First we had to convince the project team, including the engineers, that it could work. Where do you draw the lot line? How do you drain it? How is the grading contractor ever going to grade these things? In the end, even the bulldozer operators were on board, taking great pride in their skill at sculpting these shapes."

Eight builders were selected to produce houses in a diversity of styles and neighborhoods. The housing is clustered to preserve more than half the property as open space. The 44 miles (71 km) of pathways and trails that traverse Santaluz's hills and valleys provide a sense of connection and community. With the construction of privacy walls and fences being highly restricted, homeowners rely on siting and landscaping to maintain privacy.

A community with a land plan and architecture to which people are not accustomed is, indeed, a development challenge. As Terry Randall, DMB vice president, says: "The architectural requirements and styling—the humble, low-profile, predominantly one-story dwellings—were a huge risk. Many of the builders from the surrounding area said to us: 'We're tearing down what you want us to build.' But we found a fresh way to interpret early adobe ranch houses. The indoor/outdoor, courtyard-style home is completely in sync with the way people want to live here in southern California."

Project Data

Web Site www.santaluz.com

Site Area **3,800 acres (1,537 ha)**

Facilities

19,000-square-foot (1,765 m²) recreation center

35,000-square-foot (3,252 m²) golf club-house and spa

18-hole golf course

836 single-family houses

11-acre (4.45 ha) village green

Land Uses **housing, open space, indoor recreation center, golf club-house and spa, golf course**

Completion Date **2005**

Even though it resulted in fewer housing units, the DMB/Woodrow land plan created significantly higher value than could have been achieved with the originally permitted plan. Santaluz dominates San Diego's high-end golf-community market, and house prices have escalated nearly 50 percent since the project's inception. Also, Santaluz has substantially contributed to the surrounding community, including funding approximately $101 million in infrastructure and community facilities. In cooperation with the city of San Diego, Santaluz is building 178 multifamily units for low- and moderate-income buyers, one-third of which will be located within Santaluz.

VILLE PLÁCIDO DOMINGO

Acapulco, Mexico

Devastating displays of natural destruction—tsunamis, earthquakes, mudslides, tornadoes, hurricanes, floods—have a way of highlighting social and material inequities in societies. At the same time, they also elicit generous responses and corrective action. Ville Plácido Domingo presents just such a case.

When Hurricane Paulina swept inland in October 1997, one of the hardest-hit locales was Acapulco. The all-important tourism industry was devastated for about two weeks, while the suffering experienced by the people who serviced that industry—people who lived inland in makeshift squatter housing built on hillsides, riversides, and other marginal land—lasted for months thereafter. Landslides, floods, and 290-kilometer-per-hour (180 mph) winds left 400,000 people homeless and 400 dead in Acapulco alone.

After providing emergency relief (and engaging in political recriminations), the government responded by designating a 6.8-hectare (16.8 ac) area in La Venta, 13 kilometers (8 mi) inland from Acapulco, as provisional quarters for 650 households. Federal and state funding and services were stretched beyond their limits, prompting the Social Foundation of Anáhuac University to step in to help. The Catholic university's foundation had helped the victims of the 1985 Mexico City earthquake, and the organizational structure it had established for disaster response was intact. World-famous tenor Plácido Domingo had been instrumental in funding and fund-raising for the foundation's work in the aftermath of the earthquake, and this time he again pledged to underwrite some of the cost of building a new community for the destitute victims of Hurricane Paulina.

The foundation sought the assistance of its university's school of architecture, which contacted one of its graduates, Carlos Garciavélez y Cortazar, vice president of design at Casas Geo. Since 1975, Casas Geo, a Mexico City–based developer of new communities, had built 230,000 units of affordable housing for 1.1 million people throughout Mexico and in Chile. Constructed of low-cost concrete blocks and built with local labor, a Casas Geo house is in the 40- to 80-square-meter (430 to 860 sf) range. Marketed to families with household incomes in the $20,000 to $30,000 range, the houses sell for an average $20,000, ranging from $13,000 to $30,000. Casas Geo provides planning, design, construction, and other real estate services, such as buyer-financing.

The brief for the development of Ville Plácido Domingo was straightforward: 650 low-cost housing units and community facilities that would serve a population of 10,000 made up of residents of the project and the surrounding area. The community facilities that were provided include a kindergarten, an elementary school, a high school, a church, a 150-bed hospital, a sewage treatment plant, a water reservoir, a commercial center, and a zone for microindustry startups (for example, an iguana-farming operation). Building started in January 1999.

Development Team

Owners/Developers

Casas Geo
Mexico City, Mexico

CIDECO-Anáhuac
Acapulco, Mexico

Architect

Carlos Garciavélez y Cortazar

The Social Foundation of Anáhuac University sponsored 300 of the housing units, which are located in a zone called CIDECO-Acapulco. Two types of houses—a small Plácido model and a larger patio house—are offered at CIDECO. The $11,000, 60-square-meter (646 sf) Plácido model has an 80-square-meter (861 sf) lot. The $13,000 patio model has a 130-square-meter (1,400 sf) lot. Both models feature two bedrooms, which open on a walled, landscaped courtyard, and one bath. Deep roof overhangs, awnings, clay roof tiles, and natural roof ventilation provide passive cooling. The CIDECO zone has a density of 36 units per hectare (15 per ac) and, with 4.5 persons per household, a population density of 162 people per hectare (66 per ac). Two other housing zones—Valle del Palmar (Valley of the Palms) and Paraiso Acapulco (Acapulco Paradise)—offer larger houses, many of which are two stories and some of which are sited around communal swimming pools.

Access to private funding is limited in Mexico. Financing was provided through savings programs sponsored by the federal government that resemble a cross between a credit union and the U.S. social security system. The federal government sponsors three savings programs—one for private sector employees, one for public sector employees, and one for military personnel—to which subscribers contribute through payroll withholding. Subscribers can obtain housing loans, which the programs pay directly to the builder, reducing the builder's financial risk.

Ville Plácido Domingo may have been named for one altruistic individual, but it was developed through the combined efforts of many individuals and organizations, generous donations of money and expertise, and federal financing. It stands as a superb example of people in the development industry responding expeditiously and effectively to a region's shared disaster.

Project Data

Site Area **6.8 hectares (16.8 ac)**

Facilities

7,636 square meters (82,193 sf) total area

650 residential units

Land Uses **new community for families displaced by hurricane; includes housing, schools, a church, a commercial center, a hospital, and a sewage treatment plant**

Completion Date **July 2001**

Jury Statement

Having produced annually more than 30,000 units of housing throughout Mexico and Central America, Casas Geo, a Mexico-based development company, has built 650 units of housing, using an innovative building system, in a poverty-stricken area inland from Acapulco. Named for opera singer Plácido Domingo, who donated 150 units, the community has provided a pleasant, secure, and permanent abode for families displaced by the 1997 devastation of Hurricane Paulina.

CIVIC/SPECIAL

CIVIC/SPECIAL · WINNER

34TH STREET STREETSCAPE PROGRAM

New York, New York

It is not altogether fanciful to think of the ongoing revitalization of 34th Street as a modern-day *Miracle on 34th Street*. In fact, the 1947 movie's Macy's department store is still a part of the scene, and the kind of holiday retail action portrayed in the movie takes place year round. Much of the credit for making 34th Street relevant to life in today's Manhattan belongs to the streetscape program of the neighborhood's business improvement district (BID).

The 34th Street district takes in the southern parts of Hell's Kitchen and the Garment District and the northern part of Chelsea, and includes the Empire State Building to the east and Penn Station/Madison Square Garden to the west—in all, approximately 36 million square feet (3.4 million m²) of commercial space. At its decades-long peak, the area was famed as a shopping destination for New Yorkers and visitors. For much of the 20th century, however, it was Manhattan's backyard, where land uses that New Yorkers would not countenance in their frontyard were allowed. Even as the city rebounded from near bankruptcy and the garbage strikes of the early 1980s, the blocks west of Seventh Avenue, beset by the familiar cycle of retail flight and urban decline, lagged behind. People still came to the area—midtown workers arriving at Penn Station, drivers using Lincoln Tunnel, tourists visiting the Empire State Building, people attending events at Madison Square Garden—but most left as fast as they could.

Prompted by the scheduling of the 1992 Democratic National Convention at Madison Square Garden, commercial property owners and tenants formed a BID, the 34th Street Partnership, covering the blocks north and south of 34th Street between Park and Tenth Avenues, through which they sought to capture the district's consumer-laden traffic. One of its founders was Daniel A. Biederman, who had helped found two earlier New York City BIDs—the Bryant Park Restoration Corporation and the Grand Central Partnership—and who, for many years, also directed these organizations simultaneously.

A major goal of the BID was to create safe, litter-free, and well-lighted streets in order to transform the neighborhood into an exciting destination and profitable retail district. In 1994, the BID embarked on an ambitious program to replace every streetscape element with distinctive, coordinated, high-quality/low-maintenance elements. Borrowing from the success of the restoration of Bryant Park, the BID upgraded two concrete wastelands on Broadway north and south of 34th Street—Herald and Greeley Squares—into green havens for shoppers, workers, and residents. These two small parks account for annual BID revenues of $300,000 from concessionaires, advertisers, and special events.

Development Team

Owner/Developer

34th Street Partnership
New York, New York
www.urbanmgt.com

Project Data

Web Site

www.34thStreet.org

Site Area **31 blocks**

Facilities **35 million square feet
(3.25 million m²) total area**

Land Uses **mixed high-density
urban district featuring retail, recreational, and transportation uses**

Completion Date

ongoing (started 1994)

Jury Statement

The 34th Street Partnership business
improvement district (BID), encom-
passing 31 blocks in midtown Manhattan, has been upgrading its
streetscape for more than ten years.
Implementation of the improvement
strategy, now in its third generation,
has helped to brand the 34th Street
district as a vital retail and entertainment district, and property owners
are enjoying increased value and
greater consumer and tourist interest.

Like most BIDs in North America, the 34th Street Partnership is a special benefit district based on an added tax on commercial square footage that is returned by the city to the BID. The idea behind this concept is that the BID's investments in the district will enhance the value of the properties and raise the sales volume and profits of local businesses, thereby generating greater tax income for the city. The 34th Street Partnership's initial annual assessment was $.187 per square foot ($2.01 per m²) on a total of 30 million square feet (2.8 million m²). In 2004, 12 years later, the BID's budget was $8.9 million. Proceeds from $24 million in tax-exempt capital improvements bonds that were issued by the BID in 1993 (and refinanced in 2003) have funded the BID's streetscape program. Annual debt service on the bonds, which is about $1.7 million, is paid from the operating budget.

Based on an analysis of typical streetscape elements, an in-house design team developed practical and aesthetically appropriate elements for the 34th Street district and in-house staff continues to custom-design all the BID's streetscape elements. In order to raise brand awareness, liberal use is made of the 34th Street logo. To date, the streetscape program has installed 450 sidewalk planters, 303 light poles, 200 illuminated street signs, 285 parking signs, 200 litter receptacles, 150 trees and tree pits, 125 hanging baskets, 97 granite curb upgrades with curb cuts, 57 bicycle racks, 37 benches, 34 wayfinding signs, six information kiosks, and five mobile information carts—all bearing the distinctive logo. These improvements, however, are only the physical manifestations of the 34th Street Partnership's strategy. The true markers of this district's rebirth are its newfound safety, cleanliness, and vitality.

THE CHAUTAUQUA INSTITUTION

Chautauqua, New York

If the physical archetype for traditional neighborhood developments (TNDs) in the United States is colonial Charleston, Savannah, or Annapolis, the holistic prototype has always been Chautauqua. Founded in 1874 on Lake Chautauqua in southwestern New York state by two Methodist ministers as a summer retreat for Sunday-school teachers, it has grown to be ecumenical in its religious, cultural, educational, and recreational programs, and it has grown in size as well, from 129 acres (52 ha) at the beginning to 600 acres (243 ha) today. "Chautauqua," a Seneca word meaning "one has taken the fish out there," soon came to mean leisure time adult education with a somewhat evangelistic but nondenominational fervor, and today it means, more broadly, a retreat from daily life for reflection, discussion, and instruction in the company of like-minded people.

The popularity of programs offered at Chautauqua spawned traveling "tent" chautauquas—a phenomenon that Theodore Roosevelt called "the most American thing in America." In more recent times, Chautauqua has served as a spiritual model for the first generation of TNDs. Seaside (in Seaside, Florida) sought to replicate its old-time summer-place feel. Harbor Town (in Memphis, Tennessee; see page 100) modeled its concept of a diverse mix of incomes after early Chautauqua. And Celebration (in Celebration, Florida) borrowed its ideal of lifelong education. Chautauqua was a pioneer for a number of initiatives in education, including correspondence courses, extension schools (it originated programs for librarians, ministers, and educators), and summer schools (Syracuse University and New York University held summer schools at Chautauqua in the early 1900s). Swimming, boating, and other outdoor recreation have always been a key element in the community. It helped popularize croquet, tennis, lawn bowling, and golf in the United States. It organized one of the first well-known day camps for children.

At first, one arrived at Chautauqua by lake steamer, then by trolleys served by trains. Houses or tents were erected on 40-by-50-foot (12×15 m) lots along newly laid-out streets. Most of the community's small wooden houses were built, improved, and winterized by their owners, while public buildings—including the 5,000-seat, roofed Bratton Theater (an amphitheater) and the 158-room Athenaeum Hotel—were designed by architects. In 1989, Chautauqua was listed as a National Historic Landmark.

Reflecting its founding in the pre-car age, Chautauqua is a walkable community. Its streets are narrow. Two main cross streets at the center of town are paved in brick and restricted to pedestrian use. Cars may be used only for loading, unloading, and handicapped access. The population density within its cen-

Development Team

Sponsor

The Chautauqua Institution
Chautauqua, New York
www.chautauqua-inst.org

Consultants

EDAW, Inc.
San Francisco, California
www.edaw.com

H3 Hardy Collaboration
Architecture, LLC
New York, New York
www.h3hc.com

Urban Design Associates
Pittsburgh, Pennsylvania
www.urbandesignassociates.com

Mitchell P. Kurtz Architects
New York, New York
www.mkapc.com

Permar, Inc.
Charleston, South Carolina

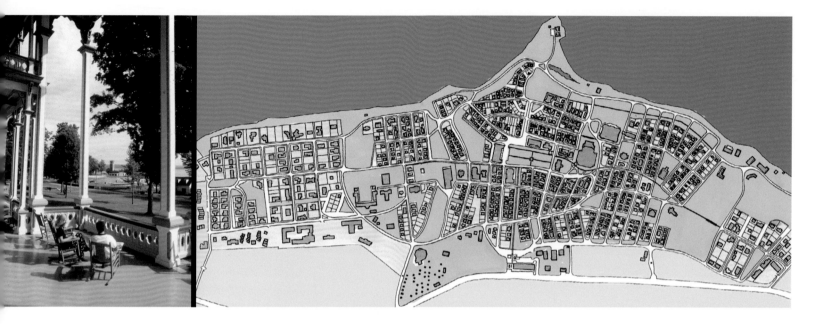

Project Data

Web Site **www.chautauqua-inst.org**

Site Area **600 acres (243 ha)**

Land Uses

summer community for up to 7,500 residents (and 2,400 visitors on any given day) offering recreational, cultural, religious, and educational facilities

Founding Date **1874**

Jury Statement

As a Heritage Award winner, the Chautauqua Institution has attained the highest standards in land use practice. The uniquely American community, founded in 1874, mixes the arts, education, recreation, and religion in an archetypal village setting that has become a prototype for modern-day traditional neighborhood developments.

tral 129-acre (52 ha) core, where more than three-fourths of Chautauquans live, is a high 47 persons per acre (116 per ha). (New York City has only 37 people per acre/91 per hectare.) Parking is very limited here, and the scarcer the parking, the higher the residential property values.

The Chautauqua Institution, a nonprofit organization with quasi-governmental powers and a full-time staff, oversees the community—its water and sewer systems, police and fire services, recreational facilities, and other public services. It also directs Chautauqua's cultural and educational programs—totaling some 2,100 events and 150,000 day-guests during the nine-week summer season, and 7,500 residents on any given day. The institute regulates construction activity through deed covenants, and governs land use and building design by reviewing building applications before forwarding them for approval by the local jurisdiction. Its land use and design guidelines are constantly being revised to serve an evolving town in an evolving society. Most recently, for example, the institute has put more emphasis on ecological and environmental concerns while continuing its focus on the community's historic character and integrity. In addition to governance, the Chautauqua Institution owns and manages community land and buildings, while individuals own the houses and guest lodge properties.

Chautauqua is a gated community, but the gates serve only as ticket offices for cultural programs and to control parking, which is limited to the outskirts, and thus they do not violate the inclusive spirit of the community. Unlike educational and cultural attractions like historic Williamsburg that focus on historic interpretation, Chautauqua, which began life in the 19th century, is an evolving 21st-century community. Its appeal derives not from its historical quaintness but from its relevance to life today.

ENVIRONMENTAL TECHNOLOGICAL CENTER

Madrid, Spain

The conversion of Madrid's main waste-recycling plant into a center for learning about recycling and environmental preservation, the Environmental Technological Center (Centro Tecnológico Medioambiental), and the transformation of the city's main garbage dump into a forested park (Parque Forestal) have transformed an unsightly 100-hectare (247 ac) land use into a community asset.

The Environmental Technological Center is a contemporary, two-story 2,500-square-meter (26,910 sf) building conceived as two wood cubes connected by a cube made of glass. The larger of the two wood cubes contains an exhibition area featuring three connected halls. The smaller wood cube contains a 200-person conference hall, administrative offices, a boardroom, a library, and back-room space. Built on the foundations of the former recycling plant, the center reuses the plant's unloading pits for exhibition space and the library.

In 2000, the city of Madrid closed down the waste facility, after having built a new state-of-the-art recycling plant and dump 15 kilometers (9.3 mi) farther southeast from the city center. Acting as developer for the project, the city council (Ayuntamiento de Madrid) sponsored a competition for the recovery and transformation of the old waste-recycling plant and garbage dump.

A team led by architect Israel Alba Ramis and including several engineers won the competition. Its design for the building focused on using materials that were both contextual and environmentally sound. The facade's plywood panels, for example, relate the building to the park. And the corrugated-steel panels used for the base relate it to the site's industrial (waste-recycling) history. The project's adherence to green-building principles reinforces the city's goals of protecting and enhancing environmental resources and providing a showcase for recycling practices and environmental preservation.

"The Environmental Technological Center is itself a recycled object, inserted into surroundings that historically have been used for waste disposal and today are dedicated to advancing environmental education and waste recycling," says Alba. "The center is a bridge between the past and the future, as well as a visible 'gate' that welcomes the public to an environmentally rehabilitated area that was once both contaminated and inaccessible. The people of Madrid now have a new place where they can learn about the environment and a new forest park to enjoy."

Development Team

Owner/Developer

**Ayuntamiento de Madrid
(City Council)
Madrid, Spain
www.munimadrid.es**

Architect

**Israel Alba Ramis
Madrid, Spain**

Project Data

Site Area

100 hectares (247 ac)

Facilities

**2,500 square meters (26,910 sf) total
building area**

Land Uses

**exhibition space, conference hall,
library, park**

Completion Date

May 2003

FEDERATION SQUARE

Melbourne, Australia

Development Team

Owner/Developer

**Federation Square Management
Melbourne, Australia
www.fedsq.com**

Architects

**Lab architecture studio/
Bates Smart Architects
Melbourne, Australia
www.labarchitecture.com**

Landscape Architect

**Karres en Brands
Hilversum, The Netherlands**

Cities around the world are finding that many large sites, such as railyards, that are occupied by hard-to-relocate infrastructure can be roofed over to create new usable space for civic functions. Roofing over is not a new trend, but it is an accelerating one as cities are forced to be more efficient with their most finite asset—land. Millennium Park in Chicago (see page 135) is one such example, and so is Federation Square.

Melbourne has always felt the need for a grand civic square, which was promised—but never delivered—in the 1837 plan for the new town on the River Yarra. Federation Square finally meets this need, creates a new gateway to the heart of the city, and completes the family of welcoming institutions—the Flinders Street train station and St. Paul's cathedral—that occupy the intersection of Flinders and Swanston Streets. On the southeast corner of this intersection, Federation Square replaces the Jolimont railyard that served Flinders Street station and an offensive eyesore, the "Gas and Fuel" towers—land uses that additionally created a barrier between the center of the city and the Yarra.

The opportunity for creating a civic square on this site came knocking in the 1990s when improved railway technologies made obsolete some of the railyard's physical plant. Schemes for the development of a civic square above the Jolimont railyard had been discussed since the 1920s, but this time the talk among state and city officials about actually moving ahead—perhaps the ninth such proposal for the site in the 20th century—gained momentum with the completion of an international design and concept competition in 1997 that was won by a team made up of the Lab architecture studio (then based in London) and a local firm, Bates Smart Architects.

There ensued a two-year-long controversy in which alterations were imposed on the winning design. Compromises at best, the changes satisfied neither the public nor the designers. In 1999, when a comprehensive review suggested—to no one's surprise—that the project, which had not yet begun, was behind schedule and over budget, the state of Victoria established a quasi-public agency, Federation Square Management, to oversee the development of the square and to operate it in perpetuity. A fixed construction budget of AU$450 million (US$297 million) was established and the agency was given the authority to leverage private funds with that money.

Opened in 2002, Federation Square completes an institutional and commercial center that celebrates Melbourne's history and culture. It features an open-air amphitheater that can accommodate as many as 35,000 people, with a stage area that is backed by a giant video screen. The 3.6-hectare (8.9 ac) space is

designed to accommodate a number of simultaneous activities. The entire deck—believed to be the largest railway deck in Australia—sits on vibration-absorbing coils to shield the above-deck facilities from the active rail operations beneath. A large passive cooling system—40 meters long by 40 meters wide and four meters deep (131×131×13 ft)—sits under the plaza and acts as a heat sink for a glazed atrium above the plaza. Its cooling performance is equivalent to that of conventional air conditioning, but it uses only 10 percent of the electricity.

The plaza is surrounded by irregularly shaped buildings, which the plaza designers, referring to the architectonic volumes as well as the surface motifs, call "shards." (This nomenclature, used both pejoratively and approvingly, has stuck.) The shards—museums, art galleries, performing-arts venues, offices, cinemas, studios, and restaurants—contain 44,000 square meters (473,600 sf) of interior space. Running between the shards is open space totaling 17,500 square meters (188,375 sf) leading to plazas, to adjoining streets, and to the River Yarra walkway.

Federation Square opened too late to celebrate the centenary of Australia's federation, but it has otherwise met and exceeded projections for use and revenues. Up to 1,000 events attract 7 million visitors annually and generate AU$100 million (US$76 million) for institutions and commercial tenants in the area. Most of all, Federation Square has given Melbournians a long-awaited monument to their urbanity.

Project Data

Web Site

www.federationsquare.com.au

Site Area 3.6 hectares (8.9 ac)

Facilities

44,000 square meters (473,600 sf)
total building area

Land Uses civic square, open-air
amphitheater, associated cultural and
retail facilities

Completion Date

October 2002

Jury Statement

Overcoming a controversial planning and implementation history, Federation Square has become a popular and commercially successful civic square for the city of Melbourne and the state of Victoria. This public/private initiative has built over an active railyard a 3.6-hectare (8.9 ac) cultural destination that can accommodate 35,000 people in an open-air amphitheater and provides 44,000 square meters (473,600 sf) of commercial and cultural space.

MILLENNIUM PARK

Chicago, Illinois

The air rights over many intown railyards have been converted to a better land use. The development of Madison Square Garden above the Pennsylvania Railroad tracks in Manhattan is an early example. Federation Square in Melbourne, Australia (see page 130), is a recent example and Millennium Park is another, but one with a distinguishing difference: It created the first green-roofed railyard in the world. Millennium Park has also introduced an innovative model for the private financing of a public project.

The Millennium Park site was the unfinished 24.5-acre (9.9 ha) northwest corner of the 320-acre (129 ha) Grant Park, a 1922 Beaux Arts design by Edward Bennett—coauthor with Daniel Burnham of the milestone *Plan of Chicago* (1909). Its below-street-level trench serving Illinois Central's commuter-rail tracks made a poor neighbor for the Art Institute of Chicago to the south. In 1998, as part of Mayor Richard M. Daley's campaign to make Chicago's motto, *Urbs in Horto* (City in a Garden), a reality, the city obtained the air rights above the railyards. The plan was to roof over the tracks with a parking garage and develop a park atop the roof slab.

Skidmore, Owings & Merrill had been commissioned to design a plan that would continue the original Grant Park scheme. After work had begun on the enabling infrastructure for the park, an adjacent 1,800-space underground garage and an additional five acres (2 ha) became available, causing the city to reexamine the park plan and funding program to take advantage of the new opportunities.

A fund-raising flurry ensued. John Bryan, former chair and CEO of the Sara Lee Corporation in Chicago, pledged to raise $30 million. The Pritzker family, sponsors of the Pritzker Prize for Architecture, pledged $15 million if the 1989 prize winner, Frank Gehry, would design a music pavilion for the park. The Frank Gehry association brought forth more gifts, and a total of $145 million was raised before a design was completed. (Another $60 million had already been raised for construction of the Joan W. and Irving B. Harris Theater, an underground performing-arts theater that was incorporated into the final plan for Millennium Park.) The city bore the remaining $270 million of the project's cost. The private donor group, which registered under the name Millennium Park, Inc., has since raised an additional $25 million endowment to fund the upkeep of the park.

The completed Millennium Park is a cosmopolitan assortment of sculptural, architectural, and landscaping elements from some of the world's most accomplished designers. It includes the Jay Pritzker Music Pavilion and the subterranean Harris Theater. A Gehry-designed pedestrian bridge—a sinuous form clad in stainless-steel panels—connects the new park to the Daley Bicentennial Park across Columbus Drive.

The rest of the elements are organized axially and symmetrically to fit within the vestiges of the original Beaux Arts landscape plan. At the center is Cloud Gate, a 66-foot-long by 44-foot-wide by 33-foot-

Development Team

Owners

City of Chicago

Millennium Park, Inc.
Chicago, Illinois
www.millenniumpark.net

Development Manager

U.S. Equities Realty
Chicago, Illinois
www.usequities.com

Designers

Gehry Partners; Jaume Plensa; Anish Kapoor; Hammond Beeby Rupert & Ainge; Kathryn Gustafson; Piet Oudolf; Robert Israel; OWP&P; Skidmore, Owings & Merrill

Project Data

Web Site www.millenniumpark.net

Site Area **24.5 acres (9.9 ha)**

Completion Date **July 2004**

Jury Statement

Millennium Park offers a new model for creating a park through public/ private partnerships of city agencies, private developers, artists, and individual donors and philanthropies. Developed in the air rights above railyards, the project—24.5 acres (9.9 ha) of open space, architecturally significant buildings, and outstanding artworks atop below-grade parking—has revitalized land values along South Michigan Avenue and created another world-class park in a city whose motto is *Urbs in Horto* (City in a Garden).

high (20×13×10 m) sculpture by British artist Anish Kapoor. Popularly called "the bean" for its shape, Cloud Gate is surfaced with 168 panels of polished stainless steel and mounted on two pylons just high enough to walk under. It appears seamless as it reflects the sky above and the people below. The 16,000-square-foot (1,486 m²) McCormick Tribune Plaza is located next to Cloud Gate and close to the sidewalk. It is used for alfresco dining in the summer and as a skating rink in the winter.

Crown Fountain, designed by Jaume Plensa of Spain, pairs two 50-foot-tall (15 m) glass-block towers from which 21st-century gargoyles—ever-changing composite faces of Chicagoans displayed on LED screens—spit water out of spigots into a 230-foot-long (70 m) reflecting pool, providing a "walking-on-water" experience for visitors. A 1917 peristyle marked this northwest corner of the original Grant Park and, in homage to the Beaux Arts origins of the park plan, that peristyle has been replicated in a design from OWP&P, a local architecture firm.

Although it went over its budget and was not completed until four years after its intended opening in the millennium year 2000, Millennium Park is considered a great success. With a brave investment by the city of Chicago and Millennium Park, Inc., the development concept was broadened from completing the missing piece of Bennett's plan to creating a world-class destination. The park draws an additional 4 million tourists a year to the area. The Chicago Transit Board has authorized the financing and development of a new $213 million subway station two blocks west of the park. And much new development is occurring in its vicinity—including a 57-story condominium tower to the west; Lakeshore East, a 28-acre (11.3 ha), $2.5 billion mixed-use neighborhood, to the north; and the conversion of a landmark office building to the south into 244 condominium units.

Underneath Millennium Park, trains still shuttle commuters in and out of downtown and garages offer parking spaces for almost 4,000 cars. And true to Daniel Burnham's plan for the city of Chicago, a great park—embellished by private interests for the public good—updates Burnham's City Beautiful vision for the new millennium.

ABOUT THE JURIES

The Americas Jury

Diana Permar, Jury Chair
Charleston, South Carolina

Diana Permar is president of Permar, Inc. Her more than 30 years of real estate and resort marketing experience have provided her with a background in real estate marketing, strategic planning, and market research. Permar's clients include the developers of some of the most successful master-planned communities in the southeastern United States. She has had hands-on experience as part of the development and planning teams for the Kiawah Island Company and the Sea Pines Company.

A graduate of the University of Michigan, Permar is active in the Urban Land Institute. She has served as a trustee, as chair of ULI's Recreational Development Council, and as a member of the J.C. Nichols Prize Management Committee. She is a frequent speaker at ULI and other industry events and seminars.

Barbara Faga
Atlanta, Georgia

Barbara Faga is chair of the board of EDAW, Inc., global environmental, economic, planning, and design consultants. Faga has directed complex teams on large, time-sensitive, and award-winning projects that include preservation plans, retail projects, downtown revitalization plans, waterfront development, parks and recreation projects, land management plans, and housing and community development projects. She has worked for the cities of Atlanta, Georgia, and Alexandria, Virginia, as a landscape architect and urban designer, and her book on public consensus is scheduled to be published by Wiley in early 2006.

Educated at the Georgia Institute of Technology and Michigan State University, Faga has held numerous academic appointments and received a number of professional honors and awards. Her professional affiliations include member of the executive committee of the American Society of Landscape Architects; chair of the Landscape Architecture Foundation; cochair of the Green Ribbon Committee for Atlanta Parks, Open Space, and Greenways Plan; and chair of the Atlanta Urban Design Commission. She currently serves on ULI's Program Committee.

Richard F. Galehouse
Watertown, Massachusetts

Richard Galehouse is a principal and senior planner at Sasaki Associates, Inc., a multidisciplinary professional services firm with an international practice offering services in planning, architecture, landscape architecture, civil engineering, interior design, and graphic design. He has been with Sasaki since 1961 and has served as principal-in-charge of planning and urban design and as principal of the firm's various governing boards.

Galehouse's professional practice areas encompass mixed-use real estate development; urban planning; and new community, resort, institutional, regional, and environmental planning and design. He is a frequent contributor to *Urban Land* magazine.

A longtime ULI member, Galehouse has served on many councils, plan analysis panels, and Advisory Services panels. He is affiliated with the American Institute of Architects, the American Institute of Certified Planners, and Lambda Alpha International. Galehouse received a bachelor's degree in architecture from the University of Notre Dame and a master's degree in city and regional planning from Harvard University's Graduate School of Design.

John S. Hagestad
Irvine, California

John Hagestad is a managing partner of SARES·REGIS Group, one of the largest and most diversified real estate development companies on the West Coast. The company manages a portfolio of 15 million square feet of commercial properties and 12,000 apartments. Over the years, the firm has developed or acquired more than 35 million square feet of commercial property and 25,000 residential units.

Before he helped found SARES·REGIS in 1993, Hagestad was president of the SARES Company, a successor company to the Sammis Company, a firm that Hagestad had helped start in 1975. He began his real estate career at the Koll Company.

Hagestad is a certified public accountant and holds a bachelor's degree in business administration and a master's degree in finance from the University of Southern California. He is a member of the Urban Land Institute, the Real Estate Roundtable, the Fisher Center for Real Estate and Urban Economics, and the National Association of Industrial and Office Properties.

Lee T. Hanley
Phoenix, Arizona

Lee Hanley is a founding principal of Phoenix-based Vestar Development Company, and has been its CEO since 1989. He is currently responsible for strategic planning, capital market affiliations, and executive oversight of Vestar Development Company and Vestar Property Management.

Previously, Hanley held positions at Estes Development Company, CB Commercial, and Xerox Corporation. He is a graduate of the University of Arizona with a degree in accounting, and has served as an officer in the U.S. Marine Corps, including duty in Vietnam.

Lee is a trustee of the Urban Land Institute; serves on the boards of the Phi Gamma Delta Educational Foundation, Greater Phoenix Leadership, International Council of Shopping Centers, Lambda Alpha International, Valley Partnership, Center for Design Excellence at Arizona State University, and Valley of the Sun United Way; and is active in several other civic and cultural organizations in the Phoenix area.

Marty Jones
Boston, Massachusetts

Marty Jones is president of Corcoran Jennison Company, Inc., a full-service real estate organization with assets of more than $2.5 billion. Her responsibilities include the development and operation of a wide range of hospitality, housing, and commercial properties.

With Corcoran Jennison, Jones directed the redevelopment of the Columbia Point Housing Project, an ambitious transformation of a blighted public housing project on Boston's waterfront into mixed-income housing. In 1993, she managed the purchase of Corcoran Jennison's southeastern affiliate, Westminster Company, from Weyerhauser Corporation. She is CEO of Westminster.

A graduate of Brown University, where she received a degree in urban studies, Jones currently serves on the boards of Citizen's Housing and Planning Association and the Women's Institute for Housing and Economic Development. She is a trustee of the Urban Land Institute and vice chair of its Affordable Housing Council. She was a founding member of New England Women in Real Estate (NEWIRE) and in 2005 received NEWIRE's Leadership Award.

Isaac M. Manning
Fort Worth, Texas

Isaac Manning is president of Trinity Works, a real estate company he founded in 2002. During his more than 20 years of experience as an architect and developer, Manning has focused on public/private partnerships that have become economic development success stories, and he has acquired a global network of cross-disciplinary relationships. Trinity Works has provided development expertise on public and private sector projects in Texas, North Carolina, Missouri, and Arizona, and is developing a number of small and large mixed-use projects in Texas and South Carolina.

Manning spent 13 years at Hillwood Development Corporation, and worked as an architect for Swanke Hayden Connell Architects and CHK Architects (now Toni Gallas and Partners), both Washington, D.C.–based firms. He holds an undergraduate degree from Vanderbilt University and graduate degrees from Virginia Polytechnic Institute and State University and the Massachusetts Institute of Technology. He is a member of the American Institute of Architects and the Urban Land Institute.

James D. Motta
Fort Lauderdale, Florida

James Motta is president of the Motta Group, a firm specializing in visioning, strategic planning, operations and management, and value creation for communities throughout the United States. He has had more than 25 years of experience in community development.

Before founding the Motta Group, he was president and CEO of St. Joe/Arvida Company, the residential real estate development and services arm of the St. Joe Company. Before that, Motta was president and CEO of the Arvida Company, a community development firm.

A graduate of the University of Florida, Motta is a licensed general contractor and real estate broker, and he holds a marine captain's license. He is an active member of the Urban Land Institute, serving on its Recreational Development Council and on the executive committee of ULI's Southeast Florida District Council. Motta currently serves on the boards of two New York Stock Exchange–listed companies, Gables Residential Trust and Correctional Properties Trust.

Frank Ricks
Memphis, Tennessee

Frank Ricks is a founder and the managing principal of Looney Ricks Kiss (LRK), an architecture, interior design, planning, and environmental design research firm with a national practice that employs more than 160 staff members.

With a focus on urban renewal and redevelopment, Ricks has led his firm's involvement in projects like Harbor Town (see p. 100), Baldwin Park (Orlando, Florida), WaterColor (Seagrove Beach, Florida), and the Memphis (Tennessee) Ballpark District, all of which have won a ULI Award for Excellence. The Memphis Ballpark District, a 20-acre mixed-use development, also received the Congress for the New Urbanism's 2003 Charter Award.

Ricks is a past president of the Memphis chapter of the American Institute of Architects and is a member of the Congress for the New Urbanism. As a member of the Urban Land Institute, he serves on the Mixed-Use Development Council, has participated on Advisory Services panels, and is a frequent meeting speaker and panelist. His professional degrees are from the University of Memphis and Harvard University's Graduate School of Design.

Robert Weekley
Los Angeles, California

Robert Weekley is a partner and a member of the executive committee of Lowe Enterprises, a privately held multibillion-dollar, national real estate development, investment, asset management, and hospitality company. He has been with the firm for more than 25 years, with a focus on residential and resort facilities representing more than $1 billion of activity throughout the United States.

Before joining Lowe, Weekley was president of American Western Communities, a southern California residential developer emphasizing innovative multifamily for-sale and rental projects.

A graduate of Southern Methodist University and Harvard Business School, Weekley is involved in a variety of real estate industry, political, educational, and philanthropic endeavors and organizations.

Europe Jury

Michael Spies, Jury Cochair
London, United Kingdom

Michael Spies, a senior managing director of Tishman Speyer Properties, oversees the firm's European activities and chairs its global investment committee. Based in London, he is responsible for the firm's investments and operations in five European countries. Spies was based in Berlin from 1990 to 1994. He has successfully led the expansion of Tishman Speyer's business in Europe, which has involved the development or acquisition of more than 5 million square feet of properties exceeding $2 billion in value.

Before joining Tishman Speyer in 1989, Spies was executive vice president of the New York City Public Development Corporation (PDC), the city's primary economic development agent.

Spies graduated with honors from Princeton University and received a master's degree in city and regional planning from Harvard University's John F. Kennedy School of Government.

Jan A. de Kreij, Jury Cochair
Utrecht, The Netherlands

Jan de Kreij is CEO of Corio NV, a Euronext-listed company in the Netherlands focused on European retail investments. Before joining Corio NV, de Kreij was CEO of Rodamco NV, a global real estate investor based in Rotterdam. And before that, he headed Royal Dutch Shell Oil Company's pension fund, which, under his leadership, became one of the largest investors in real estate in the United States and Europe in the 1980s.

As a former chair of ULI's European Policy and Practice Committee and now as cochair of the ULI Europe awards jury, de Kreij is interested in sharing experiences with his U.S. counterparts. He currently holds a number of board positions in real estate and financial investment companies.

Timothy Cyr
Meudon, France

Timothy Cyr is vice president and part owner of Groupe France Terre, a residential developer that is active throughout France. The firm's activities include land development, residential construction, rental housing development, marketing, and property management for private investors. Cyr has been in the field of real estate development for nearly 20 years.

A member of the Urban Land Institute, he has been actively involved in urban renewal and now chairs ULI Europe's Urban Renewal Council.

Cyr was born in Canada. After graduating with a bachelor's degree in commerce with honors from Queen's University, he joined Coopers and Lybrand as a chartered accountant, first in Toronto and then in Paris.

Francis Duffy
London, United Kingdom

Francis Duffy founded DEGW, an international architecture practice, in 1974. He specializes in the improvement of design in working environments, and has done research and consulted in this area of practice. He has written a number of books that relate organizational and technological changes to office design, as well as books on architectural theory, practice, and design for a wider audience.

Duffy holds degrees from the Architectural Association School, the University of California at Berkeley (M.Arch.), and Princeton University (Ph.D.). He has been president of the Royal Institute of British Architects and in 1996 was knighted a Commander of the Order of the British Empire (CBE).

Ayse Hasol Erktin
Istanbul, Turkey

Ayse Hasol Erktin is a partner at HAS Architects, Ltd., a leading Turkish design/build firm, where she has been for more than 15 years, designing and coordinating various housing, office, health care, and hospitality projects. Notable projects include the five-star Swissôtel Grand Hotel Efes; and the 209-bed Anadolu Health Center. Under her leadership, HAS formed project-based associations with Skidmore, Owings & Merrill in 1993; REES Associates, Inc., in 1999; and NBBJ in 2003.

A graduate of Harvard University's Graduate School of Design, Ertkin received a master's degree in business administration from Bogazici University and a bachelor's of science in architecture from Istanbul Technical University. She is an executive committee member of the ULI Turkey Council and has served as president of the Istanbul Project Management Association and vice president of the Harvard Alumni Club of Turkey. In her writing and speaking, Ertkin focuses on the management of creativity and the value of design.

John Gómez Hall
Madrid, Spain

John Gómez Hall has been active in the real estate industry since 1960. His first company, a real estate consultancy, was involved in developments throughout Spain and in Nice and Paris. After selling his majority stake to a multinational firm in 1973, he became involved in developing office space and introducing modern for-lease distribution warehouses and logistics centers to the Madrid and Barcelona markets. He continued to work in the development and market research field with Bancaya Inmobiliaria (Banco Vizcaya Group) and a joint venture company it formed with Banco de Chile.

From 1980 to 1986, Gómez Hall carried out various business park developments in Miami and the San Francisco Bay Area, following which he joined Prima Inmobiliaria, S.A., one of Spain's largest property companies. When Vallehermoso bought Prima in 2001, Gómez Hall became an executive president and board member.

In 2003, he joined Hines as country head and later became a managing director. Gómez Hall has a degree in architecture from London University.

Gilberto Jordan
Lisbon, Portugal

Gilberto Jordan started his real estate career in 1984 and in 1996 he became managing director in the André Jordan Group, a Lisbon-based developer of resort and residential communities that has been Portugal's largest land developer for the past 30 years. In 2005, the André Jordan Group sold its marina and property business in Vilamoura—a leisure resort in the Algarve—and it now focuses on the ownership and management of Vilamoura's five championship golf courses and a golf residential development, Belas Country Club, in Lisbon.

Gilberto Jordan is on the board of a number of companies, associations, and foundations. He is vice chair of ULI Portugal and cochair of ULI Europe's Resort Development Council. He is a director of SELECTA, a real estate fund and asset management company, and serves on the board of directors of the Algarve Regional Agency for Energy and Environment and as vice president of the organizing committee of the Lisbon Real Estate Fair and Conference. He is a graduate in economics of the Technical University, Lisbon.

C.Y. Leung, Jury Chair
Hong Kong

Chun-ying Leung is chairman of
DTZ Debenham Tie Leung Asia,
a leading property services company with 125 offices in 33 countries employing more than 6,500
people worldwide. He is a past
chairman of the Royal Institution
of Chartered Surveyors and past
president of the Institute of Surveyors in Hong Kong.

Leung contributed to the adop-
tion of a framework for land use
policies and real estate development in mainland China. In 1980,
he was officially appointed as an
adviser to the land and housing
reform committees of the governments in Shanghai, Tianjin, and
Shenzhen. In 1993, his company
began operations in Shanghai and
Shenzhen, the first among over-
seas real estate consultancies
to establish operations on the
mainland.

Since 1997, Leung has been a
member of the Executive Council
of Hong Kong. In 2003, he was
elected a member of the National
Standing Committee of the Chinese People's Political Consulta-
tive Conference.

Sean Chiao
Hong Kong

Sean Chiao is an urban designer
and architect with extensive experience in the United States and
Asia. He is the regional director of
EDAW's Asia practice. As a director of multidisciplinary teams,
Chiao pioneered EDAW's unique
collaborative approach and ethos
in Asia. He has worked on master
planning new communities, the
visioning of new urban developments, major urban revitalization
projects, and the design of public
open spaces. He has helped for-
mulate policies and strategies for
urban development and implementation at the regional and local
levels, and worked with neighborhood groups on the development
of design briefs and guidelines.

Chiao's work has received
many awards, most recently, three
major awards—including one
from the American Society of
Landscape Architects—for his
master plan and landscape design
for the Jinji Lake waterfront in
Suzhou, China. Chiao earned degrees in urban design from Harvard University and the University
of California at Berkeley.

James M. DeFrancia
Aspen, Colorado

James DeFrancia is a principal
and co-owner of Lowe Enterprises,
Inc., a company engaged in residential, commercial, and resort
development activities. He leads
Lowe's national community development division. Before joining
Lowe, he held several positions
with ITT Corporation, including
president of its Levitt homebuilding subsidiary in Puerto Rico; held
executive positions with an international investment group in
Venezuela; and served as an
officer in the U.S. Navy.

DeFrancia is a ULI trustee and a
board member of Wynne/Jackson,
Inc., the Aspen Theatre in the
Park, and KAJX Public Radio, as
well as a member of the real estate board of CityNet Telecommunications, Inc. He is a past national director of the National
Association of Home Builders.

He is a graduate of the U.S.
Naval Academy. DeFrancia has
served on the Southern Growth
Policies Board, the Metropolitan
Washington Airports Authority
Board, the Virginia Commission on
Poverty, the Economic Recovery
Commission, and the advisory
councils of Shenandoah University
and the George Washington Uni-
versity.

Akio Makiyama
Tokyo, Japan

Akio Makiyama is chairman of the
Forum for Urban Development in
Tokyo, which he founded in 1984.
The purpose of the Forum is to or-
ganize large-scale, public/private
development, and it has launched
more than 20 projects globally in
the domains of business, politics,
and culture. Currently, Makiyama
is working to establish a new
institute on global governance,
which is tentatively named Forum
and Institute for Global Crisis Sim-
ulation Study (GLOCS-FORUM).

Makiyama graduated from Keio
University's faculty of engineering
in 1964. While a student, he organized his first cultural project—
the All Japanese Student Man-
dolin Orchestra Society. Working
for Mitsui & Co., Makiyama produced several projects at the 1970
Osaka World Expo and at the 1975
World Ocean Expo in Okinawa.

In 1977, he stood for national
election as a New Liberal Club
member, for which he served
as the policymaker for foreign
affairs and urban development.
Makiyama organized and chaired
the ULI Japan Council, securing
the participation of key Japanese
companies and public organizations. He has been a governor of
the ULI Foundation since 2001.

Edmund N.S. Tie
Singapore

With more than 30 years of experience in real estate consultancy, Edmund Tie is widely regarded as one of Asia's leading property experts, particularly in the areas of development and marketing and investment sales. Tie has a strong regional and industry perspective and he maintains a wide network of property owners and developers.

Formerly managing director of a leading international property consultancy in Singapore, he established Edmund Tie & Company in 1995 with 12 founding partners. By 2000, the company had expanded to 16 key cities throughout Southeast Asia and had a staff of more than 1,700. That year it merged with DTZ Holdings (Europe) and CY Leung & Company (North Asia) to form a new global entity, DTZ Debenham Tie Leung.

Tie has led many charity drives and helped raise funds exceeding $10 million—mainly for the Community Chest of the Ministry of Community Development and Sports—in recognition of which he was awarded the Public Service Medal by the Republic of Singapore in 2001.

Peter Verwer
Sydney, Australia

Peter Verwer is chief executive of the Property Council of Australia, the nation's leading advocate for investment property interests. The Property Council is an organization with more than 2,000 members—companies and individuals in the commercial real estate industry. It employs 80 people around the country and its budget exceeds AU$16 million (US$12 million). In addition to its core business of advocacy and public affairs, the Property Council operates educational programs, conducts research, publishes, and offers networking services.

Verwer's current priorities are tax reform, economic growth, and regulatory reform. He is a member of many public and private sector organizations. He is a graduate of Sydney University, where he studied philosophy.

Stephany N. Yu
Shanghai

Stephany Yu is president and CEO of Shanghai Luting Group Ltd., a development firm with projects in China, Australia, and British Columbia, Canada. She is a graduate of Shanghai Fudan University.